Praise for
A Disciple-M

"Men who want to be godly leaders in their family, business, community, or church would greatly benefit from this intense discipleship course. It is not for the faint of heart but for men who want to grow deeper in their walk with Christ and be prepared to teach others about Jesus. The Scripture memory, doctrinal studies, and real life application make this an excellent course for any individual or church."

—Bob Russell, Retired Senior Minister, Southeast Christian Church (Louisville, KY)

"The only thing better than seeing a man pursue God is seeing him do it with other men. Kurt and Eric's material will be a great blessing to all brothers who want to help each other be more like Jesus."

—Rick Atchley, Senior Minister, Richland Hills Church of Christ (Fort Worth, TX)

"Because of DC, lives have been changed for the good. There have been people in our congregation for many years who are now rejuvenated. There are those who are willing to step out in faith and get involved, where previously passivity reigned. We have quiet ones who are now praying openly with others, sharing what God is doing in their lives. Another observation is the bond that the DC groups have formed, sisterhood and brotherhood relationships where accountability is upheld and where people have a safe place to seek prayer and wisdom. It is so refreshing to witness these changes in the lives of others who are making a big difference in the church body."

—Sandy Baker, Westport Road Baptist Church (Louisville)

"We have had the wonderful experience of leading *DC:/Thoroughly Equipped* groups both in the Upper Peninsula of Michigan and in Southwest Florida. This material is relevant and challenging regardless of geography. It is exciting to see men and women grow in their relationship with God and be used by God in many ways."

—Dwight Wilkins, Administrative Pastor, New Day Christian Church (Port Charlotte, FL)

"When an average guy learns how to take his ordinary, everyday, walking around, going to work, playing with kids, hanging out with neighbors kind of life and places it daily before God…extraordinary things happen! Beyond the inspiration of a men's retreat or a weekend church service, these materials help guys get to know God on a deeply personal and consistent level."

—Mike Breaux, Teaching Pastor, Heartland Community Church (Rockford, IL)

"As a Bible college professor, I evaluate books, and this one is excellent—discerning in both scope and sequence. As a preacher, I evaluate lives. I spent a year working at Southeast Christian Church and saw firsthand the lives this book transformed. I saw the people who went through the material grow in depth, wisdom, hunger, and godliness. Thanks, Kurt and Eric, for making disciples and for making a great discipling tool."

—Matt Proctor, President, Ozark Christian College (Joplin, MO)

"Because the Christian life is a marathon, not a sprint, those who want to run the race with perseverance would be well advised to pick up *Thoroughly Equipped*. This comprehensive program of Scripture memorization, Bible reading, and doctrinal discussion has spurred many of our church members on to a deeper relationship with Jesus and closer community with others."

—Dave Stone, Senior Minister, Southeast Christian Church (Louisville)

"Our intent in starting DC was to strengthen our leadership team. The result of the first two years has far exceeded expectations. DC has been a life changing experience for each member of our leadership team. Strengthened by DC, our leadership team radiates faith, love, and harmony. And their deepened commitment to God's mission moves others to join in and energetically participate in the work of lovingly bring people to a living relationship with Jesus Christ. We so appreciate your efforts and the miraculous impact of DC. Thank you."

—Art Zoss, Mount Olive Lutheran Church (Greenwood, IN)

“As a graduate of DC, I had the opportunity to participate in and see firsthand how this curriculum changes the lives of women. The discipline of memorizing Scripture, reading through the Bible, tackling tough topics, and growing in leadership skills was profound and humbling at the same time. I would recommend DC for anyone seeking a strong Biblical foundation. It is not easy, but it is more than worth it!”

—Debbie Scheller, Women’s Ministry Team Leader, Southeast Christian Church (Louisville)

“It has been an unexpected blessing for the DC members to be able to open up and have honest and informed discussion on so many topics. Of course, some of the topics – and definitely how people really see them – are considered almost taboo in many churches. Not so in DC. When you start with the Bible, and have a basic understanding of how to read and appreciate the Scriptures, no subjects are out of bounds. More importantly, many of our ingrained ideas are exposed as weak or even unsupportable by the Word. Sections of the Bible that were incomprehensible and unexplored become the source of increased faith. Of course, other matters we thought were clear and simple have become more nuanced. One of our primary mission statements at Laurel is to be honest seekers of the truth and to encourage others on that path. DC is a great way to further that goal. Thanks for all your good work.”

—John B. Waters III, Laurel Church of Christ (Knoxville, TN)

“[DC] has been the best experience in discipleship that I've ever had. What happened in the lives of the guys I studied with and met with for these last 2+ years has been fantastic, and in my life too. We grew together in the Lord and in our love for one another. It was beyond what I dreamed of. None of these guys were used to teaching at all prior to this study. Now one of them is teaching an adult SS class and has started a ministry to married couples in our church. Another is teaching a middle school SS class. Another is a small group leader in the youth group. It's been good to see these guys grow and take on responsibility in the church.”

—Kevin Moyers, Rinehart Christian Church (Richards, MO)

"At 48 years old, I had always attended a church, but had never read the entire Bible…I was one of ten men who were in the initial DC course at Christ's Church at Mason. Since 2006, we have had seven DC groups with over 50 men completing the course. I have co-facilitated four of the seven groups. Men often ask me why I keep showing up on Sunday mornings to go through the course again and again. I tell them the reason is simple. After 25 years of attending church and Sunday School, I have finally found a comprehensive study that keeps me in The Word daily and challenges me to think through all the topics that make Christianity relevant in today's world. In addition, this course has allowed me to build life-changing relationships with other men. Thanks to the DC course, I now have a "Band of Brothers"—to go to battle as I journey through the fallen world. At Christ's Church at Mason, we tell men who inquire about the course that this is not your father's Bible study. It is Your Father's Discipleship Plan, designed especially for you. As we say often during the course, you are not graduating from church upon completion. You are "Thoroughly Equipped" to make disciples of others as our Lord and Savior Jesus has commanded us to do."

—Doug Parrott, Christ's Church at Mason (Mason, OH)

ROLL UP YOUR SLEEVES

Getting Thoroughly Equipped in a Post-Christian World

Kurt Sauder

and

Eric Schansberg

FURTHER STILL
MINISTRIES

Roll Up Your Sleeves: Getting Thoroughly Equipped in a Post-Christian World

ISBN 978-0-9845458-6-5

See: ThoroughlyEquipped.org and FurtherStillMinistries.org for information about the broader ministry. For more information, contact Eric at DSchansb@ius.edu.

Contents

One
What's the Plan? **1**

Two
Our Great Callings: the Creation Mandate and the Great Commission **19**

Three
Discipleship, Disciplines, and Making Disciple-Makers **38**

Four
Methods in Ministry: Preaching, Mentorship, and Small Groups **58**

Five
Models in Ministry: Funnels, Chairs, and Discipleship **72**

Six
A Range of Spiritual Growth Opportunities **87**

Seven
Conclusion: Opportunities and Challenges **109**

Appendix 1
Twelve Tips for Running an Effective Christian Small Group: An "Equipping Group" 120

Appendix 2
List of 200-level and 300-level book studies 124

Selected Bibliography 127

Chapter 1

What's the Plan?

But grow in the grace and knowledge of our Lord and Savior Jesus Christ. To him be glory both now and forever! Amen.

—II Peter 3:18

From Abraham to Jesus, the most important people are not priests, but shepherds, soldiers, men of property, craftsmen, housewives, queens and kinds, manservants and maidservants, fishermen, prisoners, whores, even bureaucrats.

—Wendell Berry

A prominent mega-church has bleachers in the back of their sanctuary—a wonderful metaphor for "fans" of Jesus. The fans are in the "cheap seats," not making the investment to get a better view. They might be watching, but they're beyond the outfield walls, sitting far away from the action. For many fans, the social aspects are more important than the baseball. They may be more interested in the post-game fireworks or Dollar Beer Night; the game itself is not that riveting. They might attend somewhat regularly, but it's not all that vital to them. They might get emotionally invested, at least for a time. But it doesn't impact their daily life much—and they may fall away completely if the team starts to struggle.

As Christians, we should be more than *fans*. At the least, we should be *avid* fans—or really, *followers*. People who follow every move made by the team. People who keep track of player statistics and personal stories. People who are there, even when it's drizzling and 40 degrees. But really, we should be more than followers. We should be people who *play the game*—who are fit and active; who can hit, field, and throw the ball; who excel as individuals, but play for the team. We should be on the field and ready for action!

We Want to Be…

All of us want to be better players and teammates. We want to be more loving as spouses and more patient as parents. We want to be more influential at work and in our neighborhoods. We want to have competence and confidence to minister effectively to everyone we meet. We want to be capable as mentors and small group leaders. We want to be equipped and engaged—tactful, loving, and courageous—in an increasingly post-Christian and politically-correct world. We want to be prepared for potential persecution—to handle it with grace and strength. We want to have a heart, a brain, a spine, a mouth, and a pair of hands for Jesus.

We want to be people who increasingly live out Colossians 4:5-6: "Be wise in the way you act toward outsiders; make the most of every opportunity. Let your conversation be always full of grace, seasoned with salt, so that you may know how to answer everyone." But how do we become increasingly able to deliver grace and salt, having the discernment to answer all people well, to share the Good News with our neighbor, and to build up those in the Church? How do we develop the passion and the ability to make the most of every opportunity we're given—in the workplace and in our family?

We want to be people who increasingly fulfill I Peter 3:15-16: "Always be prepared to give an answer to everyone who asks you to give the reason for the hope that you have. But do this with gentleness and respect, keeping a clear conscience, so that those who speak maliciously against your good behavior in Christ may be ashamed of their slander." How do we become impressive in word and deed, to give answers that are soaked with grace and truth, to be gentle and hope-filled, to be reasonable and respectful?

Most churches feature active ministers and relatively passive recipients. In I Corinthians 12:7, Paul writes: "Now to each one, the manifestation of the Spirit is given for the common good" But we often read this as if believers are to behave themselves, give some money, and help out here and there. We read I Peter 2:9—that we are "a chosen people, a royal priesthood, a holy nation"—as if those titles reduce to keeping out of trouble, coming to church, and handing out bulletins with a smile.

Showing up at weekend worship services and attending a Bible study; greeting people at church and holding babies; giving some money and being nice to my neighbors. These are all good things. But none of these are sufficient for being a disciple of Jesus, a Kingdom worker, or one who can make disciples who can make disciples—to fulfill God's grander designs and greater purposes for us.

In Genesis 3, we're given God's narrative of "The Fall"—Satan tempts Eve who eats the fruit. But in Genesis 3:6, we read that Adam was standing there with her while this was unfolding. Larry Crabb notes that Adam's silence wasn't golden, it was lethal. His failure to speak—his sin of omission—was devastating. God had spoken creation into existence, turning darkness and chaos into light, order and beauty. Adam stayed quiet in the face of temptation and turned God's good creation back toward darkness and chaos.

Crabb argues that the "silence of Adam" is a particular challenge for men. But for all of us, the call is to step into darkness and chaos—and work to redeem each moment, aiming for light, order and beauty. Often, this is difficult, requiring courage and competence, grace and truth.

All of us *want* these things. But good intentions are not enough. We must turn good intentions into efforts to be intentional and actions that will be effective. What is required to accomplish these goals? Dependence on God and the Holy Spirit inside of us. Relying on the example of Jesus and working to get thoroughly equipped for every opportunity we're given. Purposeful investments in a discipleship relationship with Jesus and godly mentors. Consistent efforts to grow in faith and obedience—lived out in Christian community.

In this book, we hope to inspire you with a vision of what God wants from—and for—you. But along with inspiration, you'll need a plan and you'll need to take action. If you're on the sidelines or in the bleachers, plug into what your church is already doing. Or if that's not adequate, find others who have the same goal—and prayerfully make your own path.

A Big Part of His Plan

The point of the Christian life is not merely to try to stay out of the ditch on the road to Heaven. Ephesians 2:10 tells us that we're God's "handiwork" or "workmanship"—the Greek word here, *poiema*, means a "masterpiece"—who have been created to "do good works, which God prepared for us a long time ago."

When we're saved, God doesn't just stick us on an earthly shelf. Instead, His intent is to empower us, to use us right now, to grow us into workers who can do handiwork in His Kingdom. We're part of His plan of redemption! With Good Friday, Christ said "It is Finished"—in dealing with our sin. But with Easter and Pentecost, God is saying "It has just begun"—and I'm empowering you with My Spirit to help with the plan!

In the powerful words of Romans 5:8, Paul writes: "God demonstrates his own love for us in this: While we were still sinners, Christ died for us." But verse 10 is also awesome: "For if, while we were God's enemies, we were reconciled to him through the death of his Son, *how much more, having been reconciled, shall we be saved through His life!*" Christians have been saved through Christ's death—from sin and death, to eternal life with Him. But how much more will we be saved by His life—in *this* life. After all, our eternal life *has already begun*!

Watchman Nee's *The Normal Christian Life* and Ian Thomas' *The Saving Life of Christ* are terrific books on this topic. Thomas talks at length about the Spirit-filled life. Nee lays out what should be "the norm" for the Christian life—to live an abundant life, empowered by the Holy Spirit, making a big difference in the world around us. Jesus alludes to the role of the Spirit throughout John 14-17, even to the point of saying that we will do greater things than He did (John 14:12). Since there are a lot more of us—through the Spirit, greater things can and will happen through His disciples.

In Acts 1:8, we have Jesus' final words: "But you will receive power when the Holy Spirit comes on you; and you will be my witnesses in Jerusalem, and in all Judea and Samaria, and to the ends of the earth." Then He ascends and two angels appear to ask, "Why do you stand here looking into the sky?" Note the amazing power given to them—and to us. Note their agenda—a version of the Great Commission. And note their implied activity—not standing there looking and waiting for Heaven, but to be used by God and empowered by the Spirit to do work in the Kingdom.

Matthew 16:18 takes all of this one step further, when Jesus says that the Gates of Hell "will not overcome" the Church. This is not merely a statement of God's sovereignty in protecting His Church. The implication is that the Church would be part of the plan—and would move the Kingdom *forward*—in the strength of the Blood, the Cross, the Resurrection, and the Holy Spirit. How do we become disciple-makers and Kingdom workers who can walk in the Spirit and do battle against the Sin Nature, the World, and the Devil?

How do we grow in grace and knowledge, becoming thoroughly equipped for the works which God has prepared in advance for us to do? How do we become salt to prevent rot, light in the darkness, leaven in the loaf? How do we see ourselves as aliens and pilgrims in the World—but also as citizens, soldiers, and ambassadors to the world around us? It is God's will for us to be with Jesus in Heaven and to be like Jesus on Earth. How do we become increasingly able to bring people into the Kingdom, to live as His disciples on this earth, and to make disciples and disciple-makers of those around us?

Equipping His People For Works

Paul describes our "identity in Christ" in the first half (chapters 1-3) of Ephesians, before turning to our opportunities as Christ-followers in the second half (chapters 4-6). There, after an opening charge (4:1), he starts into a long discussion of unity (4:2-16), wrapping up with an explicit call for church leaders to equip lay people in verses 11-16—so they can pursue unity…and everything else.

> [11] *So Christ himself gave the apostles, the prophets, the evangelists, the pastors and teachers,* [12] *to equip his people for works of service, so that the body of Christ may be built up* [13] *until we all reach unity in the faith and in the knowledge of the Son of God and become mature, attaining to the whole measure of the fullness of Christ.* [14] *Then we will no longer be infants, tossed back and forth by the waves, and blown here and there by every wind of teaching and by the cunning and craftiness of people in their deceitful scheming.* [15] *Instead, speaking the truth in love, we will grow to become in every respect the mature body of him who is the head, that is, Christ.* [16] *From him the whole body, joined and held together by every supporting ligament, grows and builds itself up in love, as each part does its work.*

Church leaders are to "equip" their people—individually and corporately—"for works of service." Why? "So that the body of Christ may be built up" and all believers would "reach unity in the faith and in the knowledge…and become mature." As such, they will be "attaining to the whole measure of the fullness of Christ." (Wow!) They won't be akin to infants or unstable folks who are tossed by the waves and blown by the winds of poor teaching and crafty schemes. Instead, they will be able to speak "the truth in love" and "will grow to become...the mature body" of Christ, growing and building in love as everyone works together. Those sound like awesome people and a great church!

The passage lays out a clear goal of vital importance: leaders are to "build up," so their people can "grow up." This passage is clear evidence that God sees ministry as the calling of all of His people, not simply the domain of a clerical elite. This does not diminish the professional ministers, but directs their goals—to focus on equipping others, allowing them to multiply their impact. Church leaders are to actively pursue Christlikeness for *all* individuals and for the body as a whole, not simply a group of super-spiritual people. "Each part does its work"—not just a few parts. And not just trivial work, but significant Kingdom work for all. Leaders build them up so they can "serve others" (I Peter 4:10) "for the common good" (I Corinthians 14:26).

The term for "equip" in 4:12 (or "prepare" in other translations) is *katarizeo*—a flexible term used to set a broken bone; to mend a frayed fishing net; to furnish a house; to restore something to its original condition; or to condition an athlete. The pastors are the resource—the coach, the consultant, the trainer. The people are the tool—the net, the house, the athlete. Leaders should use a process that mends and restores as necessary; establishes a foundation as appropriate; prepares people for ministry in general; and trains people for particular ministries.

What's wrong with "infants" (4:14)? It's commendable to have a child-like faith, right? But this only speaks to the child-like trust we should have in our benevolent Father. And it's one thing to *be* an infant; it's another to *remain* an infant. Children settle for milk and often don't know any better. But they should be encouraged to travel a path to maturity through discipleship of knowledge and skills, modeled through examples and relationship, relying on exhortation and patience. More people need to move from spiritual diapers to the full armor of God!

We're built to be meat-eaters, not bottle-drinkers. Paul tells us that infants lack a solid foundation and are weak in their faith; they are vulnerable to temptation and peer pressure; they lack knowledge and are easily deceived; they create disunity or contribute to it; they lack wisdom and discernment and are prone to poor judgments. In contrast, striving toward maturity implies growth, increase, building up.

One of the most difficult challenges in ministry is teaching people how to balance truth with love (4:15). Truth without love is like a rattlesnake; love without truth is like a jellyfish; one must have both to be fruitful in the Kingdom! It's all too rare for people in the Church to have this balance. In Galatians 6:1, Paul exhorts that "you who live by the Spirit" should "restore a sinner gently." It is difficult to deal with sinners gently—with grace and knowledge—and to restore them. How do we become people who can do this?

Unfortunately, church leaders routinely allow themselves to be diverted by other good tasks. Greg Ogden says, "The whole people of God are ministers, while the church staff are the administers...If I were Satan, I would distract [pastors] with other good and high-sounding activities that have nothing to do with growing people to maturity and engaging them in ministry." If they succumb to this temptation, they will fall short of Paul's call in Ephesians and our Lord's Great Commission.

A Generational Legacy

It's easy to reduce Christianity to its individualistic components. Jesus died for *my* sins. I need to accept the grace of God for *my* salvation; I can't rely on my parents to get into Heaven. I have a *personal* relationship with Jesus. God is *my* Father; Jesus is *my* Friend; Holy Spirit is *my* Counselor. All of this, particularly in a relatively individualistic American culture, lends itself to practicing "Lone Ranger Christianity." Instead, our God is Triune; our love is necessarily practiced in relationship; and our faith is bolstered in community.

This is probably easiest to see and imagine in the context of marriage and family. You can't be a spouse or an effective parent by flying solo. Parenting is both a huge opportunity and a barometer of our faith's effectiveness. For those who are married, we are called to strong marriages, to build each other up in the faith. For those with children, we are called to raise them in the faith—rather than simply getting them to behave and go to church. This leads to a generational component—a legacy, where our children hopefully raise godly children, and so on.

Of broader importance, we are called to love our neighbor—both outside and inside the Church. For those outside the Church, we are to love them, share the Good News of the Gospel with them, and invite them into the goodness of God's Kingdom. For those inside the Church, we are to aim for a spiritual legacy—to make disciples who can make disciples who can make disciples. As John says about his figurative offspring: "I have no greater joy than to hear that my children are walking in the truth." (III John 4) Beyond that, how much better is it to *see* this than merely to *hear* it? And how much greater joy is there to see that legacy to move from children to grandchildren and great-grandchildren?

II Timothy 2:2 is a beautiful expression of this calling: "And the things you have heard me say in the presence of many witnesses, entrust to reliable people who will also be qualified to teach others." There are four generations in this verse: Paul, Timothy, those qualified to teach, and those they teach. In all of this, how do we train "the next generation"—whether our children or new believers? How do we get trained to be effective multipliers and disciple-makers?

Catch the Vision and Work the Plan

In I Corinthians 9:24-27, Paul relies on an analogy to sports and training:

> *Do you not know that in a race all the runners run, but only one gets the prize? Run in such a way as to get the prize. Everyone who competes in the games goes into strict training. They do it to get a crown that will not last, but we do it to get a crown that will last forever. Therefore, I do not run like someone running aimlessly; I do not fight like a boxer beating the air. No, I strike a blow to my body and make it my slave so that after I have preached to others, I myself will not be disqualified for the prize.*

The Christian life is a high-stakes race that requires purposeful training and passionate running. If following Christ is as challenging as learning to pole vault or to play the violin, perhaps a similar level of training is appropriate for the professing disciple of Jesus. We would never dream of having our kids compete in gymnastics or ballet, soccer or football—

without training, practicing, and working with coaches. And yet, we treat the Christian life as something that can be done well with little or no commitment, effort, training, or sacrifice. How can we imagine that this approach will be successful?

Three things are required to roll up your sleeves:

1.) **a passionate *vision* for becoming a disciple and then a disciple-maker;**
2.) **a workable *plan* to fulfill the vision; and**
3.) **the resources and patience to *execute* the plan.**

What does it take for you and others to go from a nice person to a disciple-maker? From a good citizen to a Kingdom Worker? From staying out of trouble to making a profound difference as a Christian in a post-Christian world? A vision that this is desirable and feasible; a plan to accomplish the goal; and the follow-through to reach the goal.

Church leaders often lack vision for making disciples and disciple-makers—and then, of course, they fail to pass this vision along to their people. Or they have some vision, but no workable plan to disciple them well. Or they have a plan, but they find it difficult to encourage prospective disciples to travel the path they've arranged. We hope to stimulate this vision; lay out the structure for a plan; and help you execute an effective plan.

Without the vision, you or your church won't get started. Worse yet, the church may be successful at "playing church", but fail at discipleship and the Great Commission. A passion for disciple-making begins with faith in Jesus' ministry model and obedience to a robust version of the Great Commission. (We'll cover both of these in the next chapter.)

But with the vision, you need a plan—and we can help with that too. If you have vision but not a workable plan, you'll get frustrated with a few failed attempts and eventually walk away from it as "too difficult," finding some way to rationalize the failure. Or maybe you have the vision and a plan, but you don't have the patience to see it through. If you don't have a viable plan, "it" can't work—and you will revert back to complacency and mostly treading water. Begin with the end in mind; make a plan; set goals; work the plan. As the old proverb goes: "A goal without a plan is just a wish."

A Lay Leader and a Professional

Aside from a vision and a plan, we also offer testimonies to inspire your vision and present a framework for a workable plan—to become a more-effective disciple-maker in the Kingdom of God. One of the compelling aspects of our ministry is our partnership as a professional (Kurt) and a lay minister (Eric). In particular, we want to emphasize God's desire and ability to use lay people to make a big difference in the Kingdom.

Eric's background is unimpressive by Christian standards. He was raised in a nominal Christian home. His parents were not particularly active with their faith, but they got their kids to a Bible-believing church. Over the years, he's benefitted from reading a wide range of authors—most notably, C.S. Lewis and Dallas Willard. But more important: in college, Eric was greatly influenced by two wonderful Bible teachers and his dissertation advisor. The teachers awakened a love for the Bible and the advisor made a profound difference in modeling a sacrificial Christian life.

Eric is a teacher by trade—an Economics professor who loves to teach the Bible. God has opened doors for him to teach the Bible and then to lead within Kurt's Men's Ministry. Through God's providence and countless hours of teaching and ministry, through God's provision and Eric's participation, the Lord has used Eric to inspire and empower men and women. Kurt jokes that he's "paid to be good", but Eric is "good for nothing." The beauty of the joke is that you don't need to become a professional minister to be used by God to do great things in His Kingdom.

An Overview of the Book

With this chapter, we've set the table with a discussion of basic goals and an introduction to key themes. In Chapter 2, we'll talk about the two great commissions we've been given by God in Genesis 1 and Matthew 28. We'll test various definitions of "disciple" and discuss the need for purposeful growth in a process of discipleship. In Chapter 3, we'll explore Matthew 28 further, defining discipleship and connecting the term to discipline, spiritual disciplines, and coaching. We'll discuss the role of the heart, our habits, and the Holy Spirit in that discipleship.

In Chapter 4, we'll discuss the strengths and weaknesses of Preaching, Mentorship, and Small Groups—and describe the ministry of Jesus in those terms. In particular, we'll note Christ's focus on empowering their "12", engaging them in a process where they actively invest in their own discipleship. In Chapter 5, we'll discuss two helpful models of ministry, discipleship, and lay leadership development: various versions of "the funnel" and "the four chairs" of Dann Spader. In Chapter 6, we'll describe the need for levels of discipleship opportunities. Opportunities should "meet people where they're at" and range from "entry-level" studies to something like our "capstone course", *Thoroughly Equipped: A Disciple-Making Curriculum (DC)*.

In Chapter 7, we'll wrap up by discussing opportunities and challenges to making this happen. It's fitting that we publish this book on the 500th anniversary of the Reformation. It's time to reinvigorate the Reformers' call for empowered lay people—"the priesthood of all believers"—and to redouble our reliance on the Spirit and Jesus' model of ministry and discipleship.

We should also note that this book is aimed at lay people, but professional ministers are certainly welcome to read it as well. For those who want a thicker and more thorough read—focusing on the perspective of church leaders—we also have *Enough Horses in the Barn*, from which this book is distilled.

No introduction is complete without a few acknowledgements. So, we'd like to thank our families for allowing us the space to write and sacrificing time that would have been fun to spend with them. We hope we've always chosen the best over the good, but it still hurts to lose some really good times. Thanks to all of those who helped us in Men's Ministry at Southeast, including the members of Kurt's Core Leadership Team over the years. Thanks to the two original groups who piloted DC—guinea pigs whose participation in "the experiment" is still paying off huge dividends today. Thanks to those who helped with editing: Jeff Daugherty, Mike Donahue, Ann Gillette, Ben Kopacz, Mike Meyer, Jay Pierce, Michael Shaughnessy, Cam Shipley, Mike Welter, and Rich Wilcke. Thanks to Nicole Wheeler of John + Nicole Incorporated who produced the book cover—and to Eric's son Zach who took the photo. Thanks to Don Gates who inspired this version of the book and provided other input. And thanks to all who will read this book, wanting to walk as Jesus walked, minister as Jesus ministered, and make disciples and disciple-makers as Jesus did.

Two Stories to Close

You go to church most weeks and you're a nice person, but isn't there more to the Christian life? The pastor keeps encouraging me to read the Bible, but I don't know where to start. I want to share my faith at work and with my neighbors, but I'm worried that they're going to ask me difficult questions. Pray out loud with a co-worker? Lead a devotional with my kids? Provide godly counsel for someone struggling in a marriage? I can't do those things! I can hang out with a group of junior high kids, but can I disciple them? I can cook brownies and press buttons on a DVD player, but can I lead a good small group? How do I roll up my sleeves and get ready for action?

Barry: Our good friend Barry is a terrific example of what the Lord can do through lay people, using a process of making disciple-makers. He was raised in a good Christian home and accepted the gift of salvation as a child. He grew a lot spiritually, but began to struggle with pornography. At age 21, he made intentional decisions to follow a path of pleasure and to quit attending church. When he returned to church 15 years later, he was approaching the end of his third marriage—unfaithful to each spouse, deeply addicted to pornography, in complete darkness.

Barry knew he had to get right with God. In 2003, he recommitted himself to God, confessed years of sin to a Christian brother, and threw away a large pornography collection. God restored him spiritually and put him on a path of spiritual growth. He joined a variety of men's groups and then committed to *Thoroughly Equipped* ("DC") in 2007. After completing the 21 months of DC, he was asked to lead a group of men through DC. He has mentored men for 12 years and is the lead volunteer for our church's mentoring ministry. Most important, he has been married for nine years and has been completely faithful to his wife.

Barry is a parole officer by profession, but he's a Kingdom worker by vocation. A month ago, a woman approached Eric to thank him for DC—even though she hadn't gone through it. The woman said that the Lord had used Barry to save her marriage and to mentor her son—and she knew that DC had played a big role in Barry's life. It's terrific when the Lord uses DC to sharpen lay leaders. It's even better when the Lord uses DC to help people make the move from knucklehead to Kingdom worker. What's your plan to join God's great and glorious plans for your life?

Chad: Our good friend Chad was asking the same questions. He was raised in a non-Christian (good, moral, culturally-Catholic) home. He became a believer at 28 and found Cecil who mentored him over the next 9-12 months. Chad joined a few short-term studies where he had to read a book and engage in a discussion with others in a small group. Then, he jumped into our "capstone course"—*Thoroughly Equipped (DC)*—with Kurt. Throughout DC, Chad grew like a weed. After DC, he co-led a DC group. He became a deacon. He has routinely discipled men. He is a disciple-maker in his home and in his job. He has been active in all sorts of ministries—from leadership in the mentoring ministry to speaking at marriage events and Man Challenge, from radio ministry to Christian theater.

Chad is a real estate agent who is empowered by the Spirit to be a minister of the Gospel, an ambassador of God, a disciple of Jesus, and a thoroughly-equipped disciple-maker. Chad is part of what Dallas Willard calls "the divine conspiracy"—God's plan to work through everyday people to accomplish great things in His Kingdom. Won't you join him—and us—in God's great plan?

We'll lay out the vision of God's desire to use us as His ambassadors—those who faithfully represent Him and perform the work of His expanding Kingdom. God can do miracles through inept ambassadors. But His plan is far greater than that. As such, we look to the ministry of Jesus, where He equipped 12 men for a world-changing ministry. The vision, the plan, and the opportunities are the same today. Understand what God wants *from* you and *for* you. Get with others to form a plan to get "thoroughly equipped". And work with others to execute the plan. Get off the couch; roll up your sleeves; and get ready for action!

Chapter 2

Our Great Callings: The Creation Mandate and the Great Commission

For if, while we were God's enemies, we were reconciled to him through the death of his Son, how much more, having been reconciled, shall we be saved through His life!

—Romans 5:10

Can we seriously believe that God would establish a plan for us that essentially bypasses the awesome needs of present human life and leaves human character untouched?

—Dallas Willard

The call to "roll up your sleeves" is not simply an inference drawn from a handful of Bible verses. The call is not only a reasonable intuition from what's at stake and the difficulty of the challenges before us. The call goes back to God's opening commands to Adam and Eve—and culminates with Jesus' closing words to the disciples.

In the Beginning: The Creation Mandate

Our God is completely benevolent and knowledgeable—wanting what's best for us and knowing what's best for us. So, it's *always* in our best interests to follow Him and obey His perfect law that gives freedom. The Creation Mandate and the Great Commission are two huge aspects of that opportunity. First, let's consider Genesis 1:26-28.

Then God said, "Let us make mankind in our image, in our likeness, so that they may rule over the fish in the sea and the birds in the sky, over the livestock and all the wild animals, and over all the creatures that move along the ground." So God created mankind in his own image, in the image of God he created them; male and female he created them. God blessed them and said to them, "Be fruitful and increase in number; fill the earth and subdue it. Rule over the fish in the sea and the birds in the sky and over every living creature that moves on the ground."

In a nutshell, we are to exercise "dominion." The modern use of this term might make us uncomfortable. But the idea is to have lives of purpose and direction, to lead ourselves and others effectively, to steward the resources under our discretion. We are to be "fruitful" both in terms of population and at least spiritual prosperity, creating value in expanding the Kingdom. We are made in the image of a creative, Creator God. So, we are built to create and to empower others—as we have been empowered.

Genesis 1:26-28 tells us that we have been made in God's image, which has a number of other implications for life and ministry. For example, the first Creation narrative indicates that we are to:

—act with purpose (1:2)
—convert darkness and chaos into light, order, and beauty (1:2ff)
—be people whose word is good—that when it is said, it is as good as done (1:3ff; Matthew 5:37)
—work to empower others—as we have been empowered by God (1:26-28)
—pursue effective teamwork and relational community (1:26-28; Ephesians 4:11-16)
—respect the inherent value and equality of all people—and their individual differences (1:27; Galatians 3:28)
—to effectively steward "our" resources—our time, talent, and treasure—including relationships with our spouse, children, and "neighbors" (1:28; Matthew 25:14-30)
—bless God and others—as we have been blessed by God (1:28; Genesis 12:2-3)
—view ourselves as God's royal ambassadors in the world (1:28; II Corinthians 5:20)
—work and rest to fulfill our purposes and callings—as God worked (1:1-31) and rested (2:1-3)

How do we make progress in these callings? We want to have the integrity to keep our word, even when it's difficult. To be fruitful ambassadors for the Gospel and the Abundant Life we have in Christ Jesus. To step into challenging situations of darkness and chaos, with the courage, wisdom, and perseverance to work toward light, order, and beauty. God created through His "voice"; Adam spoke words of vocation before *failing* to speak in the temptation with the Devil; disciples need to "find their voices"—to speak competently into difficult contexts.

Then, in Genesis 2, mankind is given its first two institutions: work and marriage.

—How do we find purpose in our earthly work? How do we redeem our work, especially when circumstances are difficult? How do we become more fruitful at accomplishing our Kingdom work? And as a servant-leader, how do I empower others in this area?

—How do we pursue glorious marriages? How do we strengthen others so there are fewer marriages in crisis? And how do we empower disciple-makers to minister to the married people in their circles?

At the End of Jesus' Earthly Ministry: The Great Commissions

The Word of God is life-giving. The words of Jesus are important. The last words of Jesus' earthly ministry are vital. Among His last words, there are five versions of the "Great Commission." Matthew 28:19-20 is the most famous, by far—and with good reason, as we'll see. But let's start with the other four.

Mark 16:15-17: He said to them, "Go into all the world and preach the gospel to all creation. Whoever believes and is baptized will be saved, but whoever does not believe will be condemned. And these signs will accompany those who believe: In my name they will drive out demons; they will speak in new tongues…"

Luke 24:47-49: "…and repentance for the forgiveness of sins will be preached in his name to all nations, beginning at Jerusalem. You are witnesses of these things. I am going to send you what my Father has promised, but stay in the city until you have been clothed on high."

John 20:21: Again Jesus said, "Peace be with you! As the Father has sent me, I am sending you."

Acts 1:8: "But you will receive power when the Holy Spirit comes on you; and you will be my witnesses in Jerusalem, and in all Judea and Samaria, and to the ends of the earth."

Bill Hull sums them up: "Go and preach the Gospel all over the world to every person. Go in the power of the Spirit, with accompanying signs and wonders of God's power. Tell them what you have witnessed. Start at home, and work your way to the remaining world from there." But he also notes that this is akin to giving vague instructions to novice building contractors: "Go build houses; make them special, award-winning houses; here is the money; build them all over the world."

The four commissions are a good beginning and a nice overview, but the fifth provides a methodology. So, let's look at Matthew 28 again: *"Go and make disciples of all nations, baptizing them in the name of the Father and of the Son and of the Holy Spirit, and teaching them to obey everything I have commanded you. And surely I am with you always, to the very end of the age."*

The one command here? "Make disciples." And it *is* a command, not an afterthought or an option with exceptions. It is to be at the center of a believer's mission—and by extension, something for which they are to be trained by those who lead them. How can we make disciples and disciple-makers?

This brief text gives some important clues. The command to "make disciples" is modified by three phrases. First, "go" or "as you go" implies that it will be a part of daily life. As you go—as you walk and talk, as you go to work or the grocery store, as you interact with your children and your friends—make disciples. It will be intentional, but it is more a lifestyle than an event. It will be strategic, but it will be part of everyday life. It will involve your walk and your talk, but it will be more than "sharing the Gospel" or being nice to people.

Baptism—more than getting wet

Second, "baptizing them." Baptism is not just about getting wet, getting "saved", engaging in a rite, or joining a church. Baptism is about "identifying with" Christ, the indwelling Holy Spirit, and His bride—the Church. The people of Israel "were all baptized into Moses in the cloud and in the sea." (I Corinthians 10:2) They were identified with Moses as they followed him. We are to be identified with Christ, identified with His Church in Trinitarian community, and identified with a local body of believers who will help the new believer become a fervent disciple.

"Identify" is not merely an association—as in a church membership or a political party affiliation. "They all drank the same spiritual food and drank the same spiritual drink; for they drank from the spiritual rock that accompanied them, and that rock was Christ." (I Corinthians 10:3-4) They identified with Jesus Christ, the "spiritual rock" that was the source for the "living waters" that sustained them. This sounds profound! Biblically, neither baptism nor discipleship is meant to be a casual attachment.

In Romans 6, Paul makes clear that baptism is about far more than getting dunked. The act represents a burial with Christ in death, so that we would be resurrected with Christ to "live a new life". The old life is crucified "so that the body of sin might be done away with, that we should no longer be slaves to sin". As a result of this process, we can offer our bodies "to him as instruments of righteousness". All of this far exceeds participating in a rite and joining up for a membership.

What does the "new life" of a disciple look like? Early on, babies often look like their biological parents. Each child of God should bear a striking resemblance to Jesus (Acts 4:13). How will this happen? Not simply by attending church and some good Bible studies. As they grow up, children must learn how to talk with God and read His word. They will learn to abide in Christ and live in community with His people. Their heart and habits will increasingly line up with God's will. Their mind must be transformed as they develop a Biblical worldview.

Not that all disciples will look alike; every adult is different. Gifts, skills, temperament, and experiences will inform who they will be as Kingdom workers. Baptism has been referred to as "putting on the team uniform." It's not that all players on the team should be the same. Rather, it implies a unity of purpose, a penchant for teamwork, a decision to train in order to "win."

Teaching them to obey *everything*

Third, "teaching them to obey everything I have commanded you." Not some things, but *everything* He has commanded. Not just some of His commands in the Gospels, but all of them. Not just the Gospels or a few pet Scriptures, but the entire Word of God. Not just a handful of favorite doctrines and a few key issues of morality, but all aspects of righteousness and justice. Not just church attendance and putting some money in the plate, but "living sacrifices" to God. Not just being nice to people and staying out of trouble, but full-blown disciples of Jesus.

Note that the command implies some urgency. This urgency is not driven by the uncertainty of how long we will live. We don't need to make sure we're taught everything before we die, so we can pass an entrance exam at the Pearly Gates. The better inference is that both His teaching and our obedience are in our best interests—and in the best interests of those around us. The sooner we can understand God's wisdom and better way to live, then we can be increasingly comfortable in the goodness of His Kingdom and increasing effective at inviting others into that goodness.

As "baptism" can be reduced to an act, so "teaching" is often reduced to something quite modest. Imagine that Eric announces that he's going to teach you "everything about economics". Here's the plan: we'll get together in a large lecture hall once per week and he'll talk for 30 minutes about economics. Assume that he is a gifted lecturer who works hard to maximize the impact of the 30 minutes. He's able to hold your attention, explain difficult concepts, and apply the material effectively to examples and policies from everyday life. How much economics will you learn? A bit, but not much.

OK, Eric adds an invitation for you to join a smaller group that meets most weeks with a good lecturer for an hour—or even, someone who facilitates a lively discussion on economics. This will certainly be an improvement. But again, even if people accept the invitation to this second teaching opportunity, how much progress will they make toward learning everything about economics over a decade or two? More, but still not much.

Why is the pace of learning inconsistent with the goal to teach you all about economics? If you do no reading or study outside of class, you really can't learn all that much. You're not making much of an investment. There are no tests or quizzes to motivate learning. No papers and presentations to deepen knowledge and practice important skills. No personalized instruction from a tutor—or help from a mentor who walks with you as you try to put the knowledge into practice.

For many believers and many churches, this is, in essence, the primary plan to fulfill this aspect of the Great Commission. But the approach reduces to wishful thinking, a low sense of the goal, or an anemic pace. Instead, people should be exhorted and provided with opportunities to invest in their discipleship with Jesus—beyond listening to a lecturer for a half-hour or two per week. And disciples need to roll up their sleeves, taking opportunities to work closely with people who are farther along the path. Can you imagine where the Church would be today if Jesus only spent an hour per week lecturing at the disciples? They would not have been ready for action!

Effective teaching and learning requires opportunities to practice, to be tested, and to receive feedback from peers and mentors. As such, knowledge is important, but obedience is crucial. It is absurd to say we believe God, if we don't do much of anything He tells us to do—or if we keep whole areas of our lives from His influence and teachings. The extent to which you are willing to obey is a useful barometer for the depth of your relationship with Christ.

Hull says that "Teaching them to obey is the core of making disciples." But Dallas Willard asks, "Where can one find today any group of Christians with an actual plan to teach the people of their group to do everything Jesus said?" Elsewhere, he answers his own question: "We do not routinely teach those who profess allegiance to him how to do what he said was best."

Part of this is understanding what Willard calls ignorance about the "cost of *non*-discipleship"—the problems inherent in "cheap grace" and "costly faithlessness." Dietrich Bonhoeffer famously wrote about "the cost of discipleship"—and costly it is. But if God is benevolent and omniscient, then the costs of discipleship are outweighed by its benefits. Likewise, the cost of *non*-discipleship is easily overlooked, but more consequential, at least from a Kingdom mindset.

If you want to obey, then you have to know *what* to obey and *how* to obey. Isaiah 1:17 says "learn to do right." It's not enough to know what to do; one must *learn* how to do it. I John 2:3,6 says that "We know that we have come to know him if we keep his commands…This is how we know we are in him: Whoever claims to live in him must live as Jesus did." In the Great Commission, Jesus insists that obedience is crucial—and we must follow in the footsteps of the Master.

The passage in Matthew 28 concludes with Jesus promising to be with disciple-makers—always. What does this entail? He has communicated His message for godly discipleship. He has modeled His methods for effective discipleship. He has given us the promised Holy Spirit to inform and empower us for Kingdom-building discipleship. Godly outcomes always require His provision. But God graciously wants our participation as well, so get off the couch and roll up your sleeves!

The Great Omission

Willard says that our failure to do the Great Commission adequately is the "Great Omission." This omission naturally points to "the Great Disparity" between the hope for life expressed in Jesus and the actual day-to-day life of professing disciples.

Instead of Christ's plan, "historical drift" has led us to "make converts to a particular faith and practice and baptize them into church membership." This results in "vampire Christians" who only want "a little of" Christ's blood. The implications for them and the Church? Not much in terms of discipleship, disciples, or disciple-makers. Instead, frustration, inconsistency, and a big focus on behavioral adjustments. As Willard notes:

> *We always live up to our beliefs—or down to them, as the case may be. Nothing else is possible. It is the nature of belief. And the reason why clergy and others have to invest so much effort into getting people to do things is that they are working against the actual beliefs of the people they are trying to lead...A major part of this important work is coming to understand what the people we are dealing with really do believe, and not pretending—often with them—that they believe what they don't believe at all...our beliefs are the rails upon which our life runs...*

Then, Willard asks why we don't believe: "How could one actually trust him for forgiveness of sins while not trusting him for much more than that?" Romans 5:10 tells us that God wants to do so much more with our redeemed lives: "For if, while we were God's enemies, we were reconciled to him through the death of his Son, *how much more, having been reconciled, shall we be saved through his life!*" Willard again: "Can we seriously believe that God would establish a plan for us that essentially bypasses the awesome needs of present human life and leaves human character untouched? Would he leave us even temporarily marooned with no help in our kind of world, with our kinds of problems...?"

Of course not! His plan—that help—certainly involves the Great Commission and our belief in the omni-competence of Jesus: "Our commitment to Jesus can stand on no other foundation than a recognition that he is the one who knows the truth about our lives and our universe. It is not possible to trust Jesus, or anyone else, in matters where we do not believe him to be competent. We cannot pray for his help and rely on his collaboration in dealing with real-life matters we suspect might defeat his knowledge or abilities." Or in short, along with his utter benevolence, Jesus is "the smartest person who ever lived." Are we going to follow His plans for us—or not? If not, we're morons.

What Is a Disciple...*not*?

What is a disciple? Let's start with what a disciple is *not*. First, a disciple is not a reference to a casual or cultural Christianity. Given America's historical connection to Christianity, it is common for Americans to imagine that they are Christians out of tradition, from a family background, or because they are American.

Related to this, Christian Smith describes the predominant religion of this generation as "moral therapeutic deism"—a feeling-centered belief in a vague god who makes vague moral demands. Similarly, Willard observes that many professing Christians are "practicing deists." They might resist the label, but their daily lives only rely on a tepid belief in a distant, uninvolved God. Willard calls this a "bar-code faith": it is vital to believe certain key doctrines that will get them scanned into Heaven. But this limited faith makes little difference in daily life and cannot be considered "discipleship".

Second, a disciple is not merely a convert. Getting right with God and starting a relationship with Jesus are vital. But there's much more to any relationship than its start. "Fear of the Lord is the beginning of wisdom" (Proverbs 1:7). But it's only the beginning! God has much more to offer us than fire insurance and a future trip to Heaven. Jesus did more than provide us with a "Get out of jail free" card. The Great Commission instructs us to teach those who are baptized *everything* that Jesus taught us. Beyond evangelism and conversion, a biblical approach requires serious attention to discipleship, making disciples and disciple-makers. Robert Coleman notes that:

> *It is not enough to rescue the perishing, though this is imperative; nor is it sufficient to build up newborn babes in the faith of Christ, although this, too, is necessary...it is not sufficient just to get them out winning souls, as commendable as this work may be. What really counts in the ultimate perpetuation of our work is the faithfulness with which our converts go and make leaders out of their converts, not simply more followers.*

If paying for sins was His only significant mission, Jesus could have accomplished this by popping down to Earth as a man, hanging out for a week or so, hanging on a cross, popping out of the grave, and returning to Heaven. Instead, Jesus lived an everyday sort of life for 30 years and then engaged in ministry for more than three years. He showed us how to live and how to do ministry, working with His neighbors and discipling a set of friends. Even after the Resurrection, He stayed here for 40 days, teaching and instructing His disciples. It's often said that baptism was important enough that even Jesus did it. If Jesus focused on providing thorough and intentional discipleship to the 12 (and others), then the discipleship aspect of our lives is crucial as well.

Discipleship—not watered down…

Most of the time, believers will not settle for explicitly reducing the Great Commission's "disciples" to "converts." They'll acknowledge the desirability of discipleship and recognize the command to make disciples. But often, they'll make the next error—to water down the term.

We've seen this happen with the term "Christian." It's reduced to a family tradition: "I was raised Christian." Or it's connected to a broad morality: Judeo-Christian values or someone who is relatively well-behaved. Or it's a cultural connection: one gets married in the Church; has some literacy of the faith; and observes the big Christian holidays. We see this with religious faiths of other kinds. If you meet people who label themselves Jewish, Muslim, or Christian, is it cultural or religious?

Often, a religious label is merely a cultural marker that has little bearing on day-to-day life. Even if they're "believers," they're certainly not disciples in any meaningful sense. One advantage of a post-Christian society, including the possibility of at least mild persecution: people are (far) less likely to casually self-identify as Christians. People in China or Pakistan don't claim to be Christians, unless it's the most meaningful thing in their lives!

Something similar has happened to discipleship. We recognize that "Christian" is an overused, watered-down term. So, we define a disciple as a step or two above cultural affiliation and being "a good person": one who attends worship services most weeks; serves at the church; puts some money in the offering; and maybe even mentions Jesus in conversation here and there. But discipleship—at least in any meaningful form—must mean far more than this.

Jesus' ambition for His disciples was greatness in the Kingdom and a great impact on those around them. A.B. Bruce said that Jesus "desired not only to have disciples, but to have about Him men whom He might train to make disciples of others: to cast the net of divine truth into the sea of the world, and to land on the shores of the divine kingdom a great multitude of believing souls."

David Platt says "We have subtly and tragically taken this costly command of Christ to go, baptize, and teach all nations and mutated it into a comfortable call for Christians to come, be baptized, and listen in one location." Instead, discipleship is to be something that transforms lives and impacts the world around it. Or as Hull puts it: "The church continues to try to reach the world without making disciples…saying the prayer or walking down the aisle is the [starting] line rather than the [finish] line." So, what *is* a disciple? What should the race look like?

Defining Disciple

We often throw around the word disciple without a meaningful definition. So, let's work to define it. A disciple is not merely a *convert*; a disciple is not a *casual* or *cultural* Christian. A disciple is *committed* to a process by which he follows a disciple to become thoroughly equipped and actively engaged—to have *competence* and *confidence* for the relevant tasks and opportunities.

A disciple can be defined as "a follower of a mentor or teacher." "Follower" is a useful term—especially in contrast to being merely "a fan." (Kyle Idleman runs with this pairing in his excellent book, *Not a Fan*.) But a "follower" could easily imply passivity and an impersonal relationship, so it's not ideal.

Likewise, the teacher/student relationship is often construed narrowly, as a purely intellectual pursuit. Or one might picture a teacher trying to pour knowledge into a student's skull, through passive lecturing—again, far from ideal. A mentor/mentee relationship is a better way to think about discipleship, since it more clearly implies thought and action, following and teaching, activity and relationship, modeling and empowerment.

Getting more specific, we can define a disciple as a lifelong follower and learner of Jesus through a combination of 1.) "classroom" knowledge; 2.) apprenticeship training; and 3.) application through practice. A disciple implies someone who makes himself available for training to reach competence in some area. Beyond that, one gains an ability to grow without (so much) assistance and to replicate that competency in others.

So, discipleship must require persistent activity, strategic investment, and an effective discipler. Randy Pope says that it implies "a learner's personal, life commitment to a prominent teacher or master." Willard defines discipleship with Jesus as "learning from Jesus to live my life as he would live my life if he were I." Soren Kierkegaard notes that Christ "never asks for admirers, worshippers, or adherents. No, he calls disciples. It is not adherents of a teaching but followers of a life Christ is looking for."

In the Bible, the term most often translated "disciple" is *mathetes*. It's used 269 times in the New Testament, 238 of which are in the Gospels. It means a learner, an adherent, or an apprentice. We can add other inferences from the Bible. For example, Hull defines a disciple of Christ as one who:

—denies self, taking up one's cross daily and follow Jesus (Luke 9:23)

—puts Christ before self, family, stuff (Luke 14:25-35)
—commits to Christ's teachings (John 8:31)
—commits to world evangelism (Matthew 9:36-38)
—loves others as Christ loves (John 13:34-35)
—abides in Christ, obeys the Word, bears fruit, glorifies God, listens to the Spirit, has joy, and loves others (John 15:7-17)

Luke 6:40 tells us that "The student is not above the teacher, but everyone who is fully trained will be like their teacher." Howard Hendricks says we often settle for the first half of the verse: "We have too many parents and teachers who think their primary goal with a child is to rear a good boy or a good girl. But their job is to rear a good man or a good woman—that is, a self-starter...We have too many people at age 46 who are still good boys and girls."

Discipleship, Growth, and Progress

Discipleship also clearly implies consistent and purposeful growth. John 15:1-8 describes a progression: no fruit, fruit, more fruit, and much fruit—culminating in the spiritual legacy of 15:16's "fruit that will last."

II Peter 1:3-7 is another great passage on spiritual growth. Verses 3-4 describe the resources by which growth takes place. Verses 5-7 describe a never-ending ladder/circle of growth: goodness; knowledge; self-control (doing what we know); perseverance (being consistent in doing those things); godliness (moving beyond the Pharisees—from externals to internals); brotherly kindness (handling those close to us); and *agape* love (the ability to love the unlovely).

But being a disciple does not imply reaching a certain level of maturity or competence. Willard notes: "One can be a very raw and incompetent beginner and still be a disciple...You often hear being a disciple spoken of as if it were an advanced spiritual condition. Not necessarily...All they have necessarily realized at the outset of their apprenticeship to him is, *Jesus is right*." How do we pursue robust spiritual growth for ourselves and encourage it in others?

The primary goal of teaching and learning is progress—not reaching a particular level, but advancing from where one was. This recognizes the current limits of people—at least the limits they've "brought to the table." But everyone can move to an improved state. A good teacher will challenge but not frustrate—and will not (easily) settle for apathy or complacency in students.

It's common and easy to confuse outcomes with *progress toward* outcomes. For example, if a college basketball coach successfully recruits NBA-ready talent and those players go to the NBA, it's not clear how much the coach has helped them. Another coach might take more-modest players and train them into athletes who can play professionally overseas. Which one looks like a better coach? Which one *is* a better coach? Likewise, think about two universities—one that attracts high-end students (in terms of aptitude and motivation) and another that works with less-impressive students. It will be difficult to measure and determine which school is better in terms of teaching and learning.

Another important goal is empowerment—being able to do for oneself. For example, a disciple should move from absorbing a concept to applying it appropriately. It's good to learn in a Bible study. But how much better is for at least some participants to become capable of teaching and leading others. As possible, we should cultivate a vision and a passion for growth, learning, progress, and empowering others. With this vision in hand, the next question is how to work to those ends. What tools and strategies are available to us as we seek to become disciples and disciple-makers—as we roll up our sleeves and get ready for action?

Chapter 3

Discipleship, Disciplines, and Making Disciple-Makers

Train yourself to be godly. For physical training is of some value, but godliness has value for all things, holding promise for both the present life and the life to come.

—I Timothy 4:7b-8

Jesus, it must be remembered,
restricted nine-tenths of his ministry to twelve Jews...
Forming people in Christ is a slow work, so it can't be hurried;
it is an urgent work, so it can't be delayed."

—Eugene Peterson

In I Timothy 4:7b-8, Paul discusses the importance of physical and especially spiritual training: "Train yourself to be godly. For physical training is of some value, but godliness has value for all things, holding promise for both the present life and the life to come." The command indicates that spiritual training is required for successful Christian living. As with other forms of training, it should be purposeful, relatively intense, costly but beneficial, and so on.

The writer of Hebrews provides a slightly different angle, praying a blessing that God would "equip you with everything good for doing his will." (Hebrews 13:20-21) Becoming equipped certainly requires God's grace and provision, but it requires our participation as well. We need to be personally invested—and typically, we need others to come alongside of us in this training. Christian discipleship would then be the process by which mentors and disciples work together toward the goal of becoming more and more like Christ—and multiplying that impact in the lives of others. What's involved in rolling up our sleeves here?

Discipleship and Discipling

Let's start with the basics of any sort of discipleship. A discipler or mentor must have relevant knowledge and experience—more than the disciple in at least one significant area of life. A mentor should choose effective ways to communicate and be able to provide a compelling vision for progress. The disciple must have considerable trust in the mentor and his methods. Discipleship implies some level of relationship, with a significant investment in time, energy, focused effort, and diligence by both parties. In a nutshell, discipleship and growth involve "working hard" and "working smart."

Christian discipleship involves a wide variety of goals. Bill Hull points to believing, living, loving, ministering, and leading—as Jesus did. As a result, disciples will experience transformation of mind, character, relationships, service, and influence. Hull adds that disciples of Jesus will submit to teachers who teach them how to follow Jesus—to learn His words; to learn His way of ministry; to imitate his life and character; and to find and teach other disciples for Jesus.

The Great Commission is "the method." We're not merely given a *command* to make disciples, but Jesus also gave us a *model* to do it: as you go, experiencing the Spirit's indwelling in community with others, make disciples, baptizing them and teaching them to obey everything Jesus commanded. Putman and Harrington note: "Most Christians have divorced the teachings of Jesus from the methods of Jesus, and yet they expect the results of Jesus. We believe his methods are just as divine as his teachings. He showed us that the fundamental methodology in making disciples is relationships grounded in truth and love."

Parenting and Coaching

Let's run with two other analogies. First, in Deuteronomy 6:5-9, discipleship is defined using the home, as parents guide their children into spiritual truths and a deeper relationship with God. This process combines knowledge and experience, teaching and modeling, encouragement and challenge. In I Corinthians 4:15-16, Paul writes that "in Christ Jesus I became your father through the gospel. Therefore, I urge you to imitate me."

Ideally, parents have benevolent motives for their children and the ability to help them grow. (At least until their children are teenagers, parents know more than their kids!) Over time, the parents' approach moves from information to implementation, from knowledge to wisdom, from dependence to independence, from consumer to producer, and so on. If a child picks up knowledge but not wisdom, the parents have not done their job. If a child absorbs information but cannot use it, then the parenting has fallen far short. If a child is still dependent on others as an adult, then the discipleship has failed.

Second, a pastor can be compared to a coach. Hull helps to clarify the picture: "The coach doesn't play the game. He has played the game, but his purpose is to teach others to play…He demonstrates skills, develops team philosophy, and designs plays. He motivates, disciplines, aggravates, and whatever else is needed to prepare the team to play." Sounds like a good description of the ministry of Jesus with His disciples!

By comparison, a "preacher"—someone who preaches to and talks at his sheep—is not a pastor or much of a coach, *at least in his role as preacher*. Putman and Harrington invoke Ephesians 4:11-16 to make the same point: "The goal of a church leader is to equip people for works of service or ministry…so that we *all* reach unity and spiritual maturity. Some church leaders see their role as similar to that of a star athlete…But leading in the church is more like being a really good coach." The star performs, entertains, runs the show, and perhaps inspires. The coach empowers each individual to perform and to work together as a team.

It is common today to hire a "life coach", but this sort of role should be routinely fulfilled by professional ministers and thoroughly-equipped lay people. Church leaders are best seen as coaches and equippers—with lay people as the primary ministers. Church leaders should focus on teaching people how to teach; train them to do pastoral work; and set up processes to equip, empower, and engage. But ultimately, it's up to you to seek and pursue opportunities to disciple with Jesus and train as a Kingdom worker. Get in the game at your church. And if your church leaders aren't coaches, find some like-minded disciples—and hopefully, a godly mentor—and start training on your own.

Disciples and Disciplines

Not surprisingly, the character trait of "discipline" and the practice of various "disciplines" are two key concepts within discipleship. Discipline is the ability to get things done. Dallas Willard defines *a* discipline as "any activity within our power that we engage in to enable us to do what we cannot do by direct effort." So, we engage in disciplines to have the discipline to do other things. And one might impose discipline to get people to be more disciplined!

Disciplines, then, are a strategic means to greater ends. We don't do disciplines for their own sake, but to achieve other goals. Disciplines are themselves difficult, but help us do things that are more difficult or of greater importance. Disciplines can even make the greater goal relatively easy. For example, if students prepare effectively for a test, the test won't be much of a test for them.

Ideally, disciplines involve some level of "measurement," so I can assess the improvement. In lifting weights, it's always encouraging to increase the number of reps or the amount of weight—and to know that one is getting stronger. But sometimes, it's more difficult to measure: "I think I'm getting more patient, but I just yelled at my kids."

Sometimes, we take the process and the results on faith—or on the basis of others' testimony. At least initially, disciplines may seem unreasonable or we may not understand exactly why and how they work. A memorable movie example is "wax on, wax off" from *The Karate Kid*. Daniel needed to have faith in Mr. Miyagi and his methods.

Or sometimes we're training for a task we can't yet imagine. Think of the future King David training as a shepherd, including a lot of practice with stones and a slingshot. Yes, it was God's provision that allowed the victory over Goliath, but God used David's years of preparation too. An example for us: why memorize Scripture? It puts the word of God "in our hearts" and the discipline encourages me to meditate more deeply on that passage. But it often takes time to see the discipline bear fruit in our lives.

Spiritual Disciplines

What is a "*spiritual* discipline"? A spiritual discipline has a spiritual end in mind. The goal of any spiritual discipline should be to love God more passionately and to serve others more effectively.

Of course, the means might be obviously spiritual—e.g., Bible study, service, solitude. (Hull argues that solitude is the most basic and important discipline: "Without it, you will be hindered in everything else you try.") But other means can easily have a spiritual impact. For example, the act of waking up early (say, for a Bible study or to work out) will likely help me to be more disciplined, less selfish, and so on. If I'm telling my body "no"—with respect to another hour of sleep or a second slice of pie—then my body and mind are in a better position to avoid self-indulgence as I deal with everyday life.

Three examples of spiritual disciplines from Eric. First, I take notes during a sermon. Whether I use them or not, note-taking imposes a discipline on me to stay focused on the preacher's words. Second, I often close my eyes when a soloist sings a worship song. If not, I'm more prone to get distracted. Third, people often say that I'm "good with names" and ask "How do you do it?" I work hard—writing down names and studying them—and then I pray to God for help. When they hear that it involves some work, they usually say they're bad with names and change the subject. Robby Gallaty relates a similar story about gardening: people say, "You must have a green thumb." He replies, "No, I have a purple thumb and two bruised knees." His conclusion: "Hard work is required to produce a beautiful garden."

Why practice any given spiritual discipline?

The goal of a spiritual discipline is not to practice the discipline *per se*. To put it another way, spiritual disciplines have no value in and of themselves; they are only a means to various spiritual ends. So, one should engage in certain powerful "universal" spiritual disciplines—such as prayer and Bible study—and prayerfully choose other spiritual disciplines, strategically, to deal with particular circumstances.

What about more challenging opportunities and the role of spiritual disciplines? All things equal, spiritual disciplines will be more valuable in areas of weakness. In baseball, if I struggle to hit a curveball, then I should practice trying to hit curveballs, not fastballs. If I'm struggling with a passage of music, the greatest value-added is in practicing that passage, not the parts I've already mastered.

Thus, disciplines should address particular areas. Are you addicted to your car radio? Fast from it for a week or two—and see what happens. Do you struggle with anger? Commit to silence, prayer, and counting to 10 (or 20!) before you say anything. Are you often in fear and pray constantly to get out of your circumstances? This week, pray to stay in your circumstances and to have the wisdom and courage to go through your trial in a way that honors God. Do you find yourself always needing to be in control? Allow others to choose your food at a restaurant. Do you struggle with "stretching the truth"? Commit to apologizing, even when it's painful. Are you constantly on-line, even outside of work? If so, put it down (and leave it down) when you get home. Pray for wisdom, get creative, seek godly counsel, pray for strength, depend on the Spirit—and watch transformation happen.

Developing Better Reflexes

Another way to think about disciplines: to create a reflex for the desired end, especially when under pressure. When we react poorly to a difficult moment, we often say "Where did *that* come from?" A reflex has risen from the depths of our souls and reared its ugly head. Often, we blame the circumstances instead of the sin in our hearts. Instead of making excuses, we should deal with the overflow of the heart (Luke 6:43-45; Proverbs 4:23) and the relevant habits. Our goal should be to develop other-worldly habits in a Heavenly sense, leaving others to wonder "Where did *that* come from?"

In *Mere Christianity*, C.S. Lewis uses "rats in the cellar" as a metaphor for these reflexes. We might not see the rats or even know that they're there. But if we go to the cellar door quietly and turn on the lights, we'll see rats scurrying away. Lewis says when such moments happen, we're tempted to blame the lights or the moment itself, instead of being thankful for the occasion to see the rats and get to work in dealing with them.

In Matthew 26:41, Christ notes that the spirit is willing, but the body is often weak. Our hearts are in the right place, but our reflexes and habits are not. We want to do one thing, but unfortunately, we've "trained" to do something else. In contrast, Willard says that Jesus invited "people to follow him into that sort of life from which behavior such as loving one's enemies will seem like the only sensible and happy thing to do."

The goal is a Spirit-filled, Love-permeated life. Willard asks if this is difficult: "It is very hard indeed if you have not been substantially transformed in the depths of your being, in the intricacies of your thoughts, feelings, assurances, and dispositions, in such a way that you are permeated with love. Once that happens, then it is not hard. What would be hard is to act the way you acted before." How do we change our reflexes? By God's grace and our efforts in training and discipline, practice and patience.

In sports and music, this is called "muscle memory." Tony Gwynn was an excellent baseball hitter who would incessantly watch videotapes of opposing pitchers. The time to swing is so miniscule, that the body must simply know what to do—rather than thinking about it. This is a nice analogy to our spiritual walk—that our reflexes would be transformed by the Spirit and spiritual disciplines. In the heat of a difficult moment, if you have to think about it, it's usually too late!

The Christian life is meant to address the head, the heart, and the hands. You can persuade the head, but if it doesn't get to the hands, it has little if any value. If the heart doesn't follow, the head will fade anyway. You can sway the heart—and then, the hands will fall in line. But if the head doesn't follow as well, the heart will be influenced by the next experience—and the hands will falter. Ideally, disciplines address the hands which have been inspired by the head and the heart, boosting their resolve and providing rationale to the head and vision to the heart. In other words, disciplines are an essential piece of effective discipleship.

Developing Better Habits

Willard writes that our bodies are meant to become our allies within discipleship, rather than enemies or a mixed bag. He notes that the term *sarx* (used by Paul to great effect, most notably in Romans) is often translated "the flesh"—as in the flesh vs. the Spirit. But "flesh" gets readers to think about their bodies, imagining that their bodies are inherently evil. But it's not my body—rather, it's the "sin nature" (as the term is better translated) that is the problem. As such, our bodies are not evil things to be *restrained,* but potential instruments of righteousness to be *re-trained.* The ultimate goal here "is to make our body a reliable ally and resource for the spiritual life."

What is the relationship between habits and behavior? Again, Willard is helpful here:

> *The responses we make to our context without thinking are simply an expression of what our body 'knows' to do. Of course, in most situations this is good...Speaking, kitchen work, and driving about the community are things we have to think very little about as we do them. Unfortunately, this remains true when what our body 'knows to do' is wrong...But the really good news here is that the power of habit can be broken. Habits can be changed. And God will help us to change them—though he will not do it for us...*

In John 8:28-29, Jesus makes clear that His "habit" was to listen to God and to do His will: "I do nothing on my own but speak just what the Father has taught me. The one who sent me is with me; he has not left me alone, for *I always do what pleases him.*" So too with us; increasingly, our habit should be to conform our minds to God's mind, our wills to God's will, our bodies offered to God as instruments of righteousness (Romans 6:13) and living sacrifices (Romans 12:1). It may be odd to think of it this way, but love and obedience are "habits" to be cultivated.

All of us understand the importance of habits throughout life. So, why don't more people work to develop good habits? As an economist, Eric is happy to analyze this in terms of benefits and costs. All investments have present costs and future benefits; we may sacrifice now for a better life in the future.

But this can be quite difficult! People want to be in shape physically, but they don't want to work out or eat well. They want to be smart, but they don't want to do their homework and study. They have the will to win, but not the will to *prepare to* win. All of these are worthy goals. Why do we fail to engage so often?

On the benefit side, we may underestimate the value of the new state. If so, the costs of forming a good habit may not seem worth the (underestimated) benefits. On the cost side, we may perceive the costs as too high for it to be a worthwhile investment. If we lack a strategy for implementing a new habit; if we lack a mentor to provide wisdom; if we don't have a friend to help with accountability, then we may reject costly efforts to add a beneficial habit.

If a habit is truly worthwhile, then we need to see it as such. And if it is desirable, it's easy to imagine the usefulness of mentorship, community, accountability, etc. to accomplish the desired end. It takes a long time and regular investments to develop most habits—and for a habit to become a practice. As with discipleship in general, the value of a good habit must be understood and there must be a workable plan (including discipline and disciplines) to achieve the goal.

Don't Forget the Empowerment of God

When we describe disciplines and emphasize discipleship, it's tempting to reduce this to a human pursuit of God's best for our lives. Instead, it's more like a partnership. Relationship with God starts with God's provision (His "prevenient" grace), but requires our participation (accepting His grace). Within our sanctification, we're God's friends, made in His image, working with Him, empowered by His Spirit, and cooperating in the business of the Kingdom—as stewards of the time, talent, and treasure which He has given us. Here, too, it's God's provision and our participation—not a 50/50 proposition, but ideally, a 100%/100% arrangement. We work as if it depends on us—and we pray and walk in faith as if it depends wholly on Him.

Habits are part of the equation, but it can be tempting to focus on them too much—getting the discipline without the spiritual discipline. Good habits without a changed heart will lead to legalism, self-righteousness, and pride. Discipleship requires effort, but over time, we can come to see ourselves as "working for God." There is a sense in which this is true. It is God's work; we are stewards of His resources! But the larger perspective is that we're making ourselves increasingly available and able—so that God can work through us.

We are only responsible to put ourselves in a place to be transformed by God. And the process itself—while important—is not where the change occurs. Only God does the transforming. But God has designed spiritual growth to be a process—and to be done within a process. Process is a great word for it: a process requires our participation; takes time and effort; implies struggle and growth; and so on. Just like discipleship.

There is grace, but it is usually supported by effort within grace. Transformation requires God's grace, but it is not passive.

"The spirit is willing, but the flesh is weak." However, this is not meant to be passively accepted as the final verdict on our earthly lives. As Paul writes in Colossians 1:9-12,

> *We continually ask God to fill you with the knowledge of his will through all the wisdom and understanding that the Spirit gives, so that you may live a life worthy of the Lord and please him in every way: bearing fruit in every good work, growing in the knowledge of God, being strengthened with all power according to his glorious might so that you may have great endurance and patience, and giving joyful thanks to the Father, who has qualified you to share in the inheritance of his holy people in the kingdom of light.*

Once we start talking about effort, there are reasonable concerns about devolving into a works-based salvation. As Willard wryly notes: "People quickly become worried about this…But most of us would not have to worry about perfection for a few months at least." Or as Carlson and Lueken put it: "Our passivity in our spiritual growth is a hangover from the Reformation. We are afraid of turning grace into works. So instead, we turn grace into divine magic." They also point to another way in which we short-change discipleship: "…we may not be experiencing transformation, at least we are frustrated by our complacency. We are satisfied with our spiritual dissatisfaction."

Again, the goal is not the practice of spiritual disciplines, but a spiritually-disciplined or Spirit-disciplined life. Likewise, "fleeing temptation" is a popular but limited approach to avoiding sin. It is, at best, a short-run solution that deals with "fruit" rather than roots. Willard notes: "Though there no doubt are times when, man or woman, we can only run from temptation, or simply avoid the possibility, that must be regarded as a temporary expedient…It cannot change who we are." Our goals are not merely sin management, but spiritual transformation—for ourselves and others.

As such, confusion about means and ends can lead to problems. One might reduce the spiritual discipline to a duty or a legalism. Failure may result in guilt and despair; success may lead to pride, self-righteousness, and judgmentalism. We cannot let the practice of spiritual disciplines degenerate into nasty outcomes; there is no condemnation in Christ Jesus. We're not trying to raise the bar or weed out the slugs. We're trying to partner with God in His desire for us to become full-fledged heirs of the King and effective workers in His Kingdom.

More potential for confusion: we want people to be confident as they minister to others. By confidence, we don't mean self-confidence, but a God-confidence—confident in what God can do through you. This involves a transfer of God-confidence from disciple-makers to disciples.

With *Thoroughly Equipped: A Disciple-Making Curriculum (DC)*, two of our goals are tremendous growth in both knowledge and humility. Growth in knowledge often results in pride, even in spiritual matters (I Corinthians 8:1). But true knowledge will result in humility. When I'm drinking from the deep well of Scripture and wrestling with the immensity of God, I will come away with more knowledge, but also the knowledge of how little I know. Or putting it another way: I learn a lot, but I also learn that I knew less than I thought.

Even the phrase "make disciples" can cause trouble. We can't *make* disciples in one sense. Only God can do that. We can't turn people into anything. We can only invite them into a process and relationships that will allow them to disciple more effectively with Jesus. We cannot elevate programs and growth over people, as if this is some sort of manufacturing process. But the command of Jesus implies that we can (and should) strategically and energetically participate in a disciple-making process with others.

Making Disciples…or Really, Making Disciple-Makers

The narrow, explicit command of Jesus in the Great Commission is to "make disciples." As we've seen, a disciple might be defined lightly—in a manner that doesn't imply all that much. But if we recall the context of the passage, we'll remember that "baptize" means an "identification with" Jesus—an adherence to His methods, ministry, and message. And the passage says to teach them *everything* that Christ had commanded—not *some* things. Not just a casual *fan* of Jesus, but an avid *follower* and a *fervent* disciple.

Jesus didn't command evangelism *per se*, but He did call people to reproduce spiritually. Hull says that "Disciple making means developing Christians who have the desire and skill to reproduce themselves…Many Christians are spiritually sterile." If we're sterile, then we're not reproducing. If we're not reproducing, then we're not disciples.

In other words, being a "disciple" generally implies a growing ability to "make" other disciples. The exception to this would be brand new disciples: they're not in a position to pass much along at an early stage, but they're in the process. In contrast, if I *think* I've been a disciple for a while and I'm not able to "make" disciples, then I'm under-selling what God is doing through me or I'm fooling myself about my status as a disciple.

Extending this further: the Bible calls us to multi-generational disciple-making—making disciples who can make disciples who can make disciples. In II Timothy 2:2, among Paul's last written words, he writes: "And the things you have heard me say in the presence of many witnesses entrust to reliable people who will also be qualified to teach others." In Philippians 4:9, Paul says: "Whatever you have learned or received or heard from me, or seen in me—put it into practice." And in a more obscure passage (Joel 1:3), the prophet opens with "Tell it to your children, and let your children tell it to their children, and their children to the next generation."

Or think more broadly—to the desire of Jesus that there would be more "workers for the harvest" (Luke 10:2). What does this mean? Was Christ envisioning more people to hand out bulletins and more people to hold babies? Those things are important—even vital to ministry and the functioning of the local church. But a Kingdom worker means something (much) more. For example, not just a couple who practices hospitality as they host a high school group in their home. Instead, a husband and wife who model a glorious marriage, can field challenging questions, can patiently handle difficult teens, and have a vision for making disciples who can withstand the challenges and temptations of life in and after high school.

Or more broadly still—and back to Genesis 1: in the beginning, the Triune God made us in His image—operating in intimate community, empowering us to do work in the Garden, aiming for multiplication and (properly-defined) "dominion." As a result, discipleship, Biblically speaking, must mean something that includes significant empowerment and substantive growth.

From Ordinary People to Changing the World

Jesus promised to make His disciples into "fishers of men" (Matthew 4:19) through a process of discipleship. And not just "fishers of men," but the apostles on which the Church was built then and thrives today. They were fishermen by trade—common, hard-working folks. Even in Acts, after the empowerment of the Spirit, they were still seen as "ordinary, unschooled men." (Acts 4:13)

This was not merely something for the early apostles. We are all co-workers in God's service—and more Kingdom workers are needed for the harvest (I Corinthians 3:9; Matthew 9:37-38). We are not saved by good works (Ephesians 2:8-9), but we are saved to do good works as God's masterpieces (Ephesians 2:10). We are called to make disciples who can make disciples who can make disciples (Matthew 28:18-20).

Sometimes, church leaders respond to this challenge by reaching out to those who already have leadership skills and a decent walk with Jesus (or at least, reasonably moral folks). These people can "get things done." All things equal, those attributes are fine. But far more important? A I Timothy 3 lifestyle; a Biblical worldview; being correct in life and doctrine; growing in grace and knowledge, practicing love in truth.

The job of the pastor is not simply to tweak Type A personalities—"leader types"—preparing them for works of service. He is also called to develop the Type B's and C's who can be excellent Kingdom workers. In fact, there probably aren't enough Type A's in the Church; we *need* some B's and C's too. More to the point: Kingdom worker status is not reserved simply for Type A's—and does not run as well with only Type A's.

In Luke 12:49, Christ says "I have come to bring fire on the earth, and how I wish it were already kindled!" We'll stoke the fire with more disciples and disciple-makers, including "ordinary" people. Along the same lines, as Ian Thomas notes in God's use of a burning bush as opposed to a majestic tree in Exodus 3: "any ol' bush will do." This is not a function of our skills, but our availability to God and the empowerment of the Spirit. Elton Trueblood observes that "The miracle of the early Church was that of poor sticks making a grand conflagration…Evangelism occurs when people are so enkindled by contact with the central fire of Christ that they, in turn, set others on fire."

Wendell Berry observes that, in the Bible, "From Abraham to Jesus, the most important people are not priests, but shepherds, soldiers, men of property, craftsmen, housewives, queens and kinds, manservants and maidservants, fishermen, prisoners, whores, even bureaucrats." We tend to over-rate the role of professional ministers and under-rate the role of equipped lay people who are faithful to God and available to His leading.

Russell Moore says that Jesus "shocked the system of God's people by rebuilding the temple of Israel with stones no one wanted." Then Moore asks: "What would it mean if our leadership structures in the church weren't as predictable as that of any other organization?...It would look awfully strange, but it would look no stranger than a crucified Nazarene governing the universe." What's more beautiful than a Type-B or Type-C person being used by God to do great things in His kingdom?

A Life of Multiplication

What does this mean for church leadership? Hull lays out four requirements to be a disciple-making pastor: "He is committed to placing disciple-making at the heart of the church. He commits himself to the clear identification and communication of the roles of the pastor, the people, and the discipling process. He is committed to the priesthood of all believers. He has a commitment to multiplication."

In sum, we seek to follow Jesus in a ministry of multiplication. Too often, churches are focused almost exclusively on addition: adding people, one at a time, to a large-group setting where discipleship will be largely passive, slow-going in terms of building intimacy, and focused on knowledge dissemination and emotional inspiration—but ultimately limited in its ability to foster spiritual growth. (Even worse, some churches specialize in subtraction and division!)

Becoming and making disciple-makers does not happen (well) by osmosis. It requires purposeful effort and persistence. It will require activity on the part of disciples. It will require relationship between mentees and those being mentored. It will require focused time and energy. The goal is empowering others who can replace us in our tasks; developing disciples who can disciple others; building up believers who can do Kingdom work.

The result: a thriving ministry filled with disciple-makers. An army of thoroughly equipped volunteers who can pull weeds and put out fires, but also can plant flowers, install smoke detectors, and build water towers. A troop of medics who can go beyond applying band-aids in a war zone to prescribing medicine and doing surgery. Disciples of Jesus who can mentor a high schooler with an abusive past; teach apologetics to college students; engage a neighbor who is a Jehovah's Witness; and disciple an alcoholic or a prisoner.

God promises a blessing if we steward our time, money, and energy appropriately. Proverbs 3:9-10: "Honor the Lord with your wealth, with the firstfruits of all your crops; then your barns will be filled to overflowing, and your vats will brim over with new wine." If discipleship is the top priority for you—rather than an afterthought—you will become a disciple-maker. If it is a top priority for your church leaders, then your church will overflow with disciple-makers.

If our church leaders aim for disciple-makers, they'll get disciples thrown in. They'll get faithful and loving people; evangelists and converts; tithers and servers; commitment and growth; people who live spiritually-disciplined lives; passionate worship, faithful prayer, and life-changing Bible study; strong marriages with effective parents; people "on mission" who will naturally make a difference in your community—and have a reputation for the same.

What does it take to become a disciple-maker? Confidence and competence; knowledge and humility; a vision to disciple others effectively and opportunities to do it. How does it happen? The church should help a range of people from non-believers to disciple-makers; from the lost to the lay leader. We must have a vision for getting equipped and equipping others; and must have a plan to make it happen.

Chapter 4

Methods in Ministry: Preaching, Mentorship, and Small Groups

The student is not above the teacher, but
everyone who is fully trained will be like their teacher.

—Luke 6:40

It is a gross error to suppose that
the Christian cause goes forward solely or chiefly on weekends.

—Elton Trueblood

In Genesis 2, God lays out the first two institutions—work and marriage. Our first priority is striving for obedience and finding fulfillment in our Kingdom work. For those who are married, marriage and family are among our top priorities—to cherish our spouses, to walk faithfully with them, discipling with Jesus and helping our children grow into faithful disciples of Jesus as well.

Beyond these vital roles, we find three disciple-making models in Scripture: preaching (proclamation), personal mentorship, and small-group discipleship. All three have similar goals—to communicate truth, build relationships, model godly living, empower others, and so on. Each method has strengths and weaknesses, but each can be used to promote the Good

News—for both salvation and sanctification—and to help us roll up our sleeves.

Preaching/Proclamation

Proclamation is used throughout Scripture to communicate powerful truths—from prophets to the psalms, from Moses to Jesus, from John the Baptist to the apostles. Today, we use TV, radio, the internet, worship services, and large, lecture-styled Bible studies. Mass proclamation can reach many more people, but its personal impact is limited.

Today, it is popular to emphasize preaching, but this was not a primary method for Jesus. Jesus did not neglect the crowds. But He did not work *through* the masses, seeking large-scale social or political change. In fact, those were some of the temptations offered by Satan. That said, the crowds represent a first opportunity for individuals to assess Jesus—an informal version of Jesus' invitation to "come and see." People could participate "safely"—with anonymity and without commitment—to hear a sense of life in the Kingdom that Jesus offered.

Preaching is mostly a one-way form of communication. In a large-group setting, those in the audience will be able to fix their attention on an effective speaker—hopefully. But this is difficult, even for the most disciplined audience members. Her baby is noisy; did he comb his hair; what's for lunch?

If preaching is ineffective at holding your attention, that's one problem. But great preaching leads to another problem: if the preacher is a rock star, then the church is an audience. Even imagining a best-case scenario, avid listeners are largely passive as spectators. In fact, proclamation *encourages* passivity, especially with professional speakers and worship leaders putting on "a great show." Elton Trueblood said, "Millions of supposed members are not really involved at all and, what is worse, do not think it strange that they are not." It's tempting to reduce church to theater—or at least, something best left to the professionals.

As audience diversity increases, addressing a large group becomes increasingly difficult. It is difficult to know what a larger, largely-anonymous audience needs to hear, since my knowledge of them is more limited. As a church or group gets smaller, there is increased opportunity for the speaker to interact with individuals. But preaching necessarily lacks a personal touch and is typically a shotgun manner of conveying information.

How does one craft a relevant sermon for believers and non-believers, lukewarm and passionate, old and young, married and single, and so on? It is rare that a sermon can effectively challenge a range of people. For example, if aimed at seekers and milk-drinkers, a sermon will focus on basic truths with relatively little to offer (potential) meat-eaters.

Sermons also tend to generate temporary, emotional responses. But they are quite limited in their ability to fulfill the larger goals of life change and disciple-making. A reliance on sermons for spiritual growth implicitly assumes a really low bar for "discipleship" or that discipleship will happen naturally through other means. But it's far easier to build up church attendance through fine preaching, than to build up disciples through a process of discipleship.

You may be expecting (far) too much from your preacher. Preaching can only do so much and was never meant to carry anything close to the full weight of discipleship. Intently listen to sermons and gain the nuggets that God has for you. But after that, get out of your pew, get off the couch, and make sure that you're making investments in your own discipleship.

Terrific preaching is fine, but limited and certainly not sufficient or even primary to fulfilling the Great Commission. Proclamation has its place, especially with evangelism and lower-end discipleship. Preaching is important in the life of the church, but it can only be a start—and should point people toward pursuing the greater realities. Dallas Willard asks the pertinent questions of preachers: "Does the gospel I preach and teach have a natural tendency to cause people who hear it to become full-time students of Jesus? Would those who believe it become his apprentices as a natural 'next step'?"

Of course, one should not condone bad or mediocre preaching. But in looking to fulfill the Great Commission, it's a fatal flaw for preachers or their audiences to imagine that good preaching is the key to discipleship. In a nutshell, as Bill Hull concludes: "sermons do not prepare people to live effective Christian lives."

Personal Mentorship

The Bible records many examples of mentorship to accomplish the goals of higher-end discipleship. Moses mentored Joshua to the point that he was empowered to lead the Israelites into the Promised Land. Elisha was mentored by Elijah—later receiving a double-blessing from the Lord for a ministry that was arguably more impressive (although less famous).

Paul mentored Timothy and others, devoting much of the recorded epistles to describing this aspect of his ministry—a key part of the explosive growth of the Early Church. In addition to his poignant departure from the Ephesian elders

(Acts 20), Paul exhibits great personal concern in his epistles for his mentees and peers, mentioning more than 60 people by name as friends, partners, fellow workers, teammates, and faithful helpers.

Presumably, lower-end discipleship was also a staple of ministry in Biblical times, but was not recorded in detail. Peer relationships, as with Paul and Barnabas, certainly have their place in discipleship as well—ministry partners who provide accountability, wisdom, and "iron sharpening iron." In any case, each of us should seek out Paul, Barnabas, and Timothy relationships.

Mentoring can be immensely valuable. As Willard notes, it is important to recognize the impact of past disciplers and mentors: "It is one of the major transitions of life to recognize who has taught us...and then to evaluate the results in us of their teaching." Or as Anne Lamott observes, great mentors are "marbled into us."

Mentorship will be effective, assuming a competent mentor and a willing mentee. Of course, a mentee must have a passion for learning and following in the footsteps of the mentor. The mentor must have a life worth emulating and wisdom to convey. The mentor must be able to model life and communicate wisdom effectively. Mentors have the vision to see potential in a person—what they can be—and the wisdom to recommend effective "next steps." They tolerate mistakes, immaturity, ignorance, etc.—patiently waiting and persistently working for potential to develop.

Mentorship is interactive and experiential. It is *quite* personal—both in the sense of its relational context and the relevance of the particular wisdom communicated to the mentee. Done well, mentorship will allow a mentee to stretch and grow.

A mentorship will provide knowledge and wisdom, teaching and accountability, exhortation and encouragement.

But mentorship also has its limits. In some ways, two people is too small. Discussions can devolve into repetitive, mediocre, counseling sessions. Having only two people necessarily implies less breadth in discussions and perspective. (This is akin to parenting, where it's so helpful to have other competent adults and peers coming alongside your kids.) Two may have limited accountability—fewer people to help ask the difficult questions.

It is also inherently restrictive—a personal relationship limited by the strengths, experiences, and abilities of the mentor. As such, a mentee should seek other iron-sharpening-iron mentors and friendships to supplement and complement what is learned from one mentor.

It can be difficult to break up a mentor/mentee relationship in what can become dependency or co-dependency. A mentor/mentee is also a challenging relationship to reproduce, in terms of developing mentees into mentors. *Receiving* wise counsel is a useful part of *providing* wise counsel, but here, it's easier to receive than to give. And it's easier to give than to teach others *how to* give. Few mentees will see themselves as capable of moving into the mentor seat or will be intimidated by the pressure of being the leader in a one-on-one relationship.

Finally, even when effective and reproducible, a mentor/mentee relationship is necessarily small—handling one or a few people at a time. Making significant progress requires considerable time and energy—and concentrating this on one person is a limited endeavor. Although mentors have an important role to play in spiritual formation, there are other effective models available.

Small-Group Discipleship

There is certainly a place for proclamation and mentorship. Proclamation is especially useful for those who are still ingesting milk. A weekly sermon is an opportunity to address seekers and to remind disciples of familiar truths, cast vision, and develop modest community. Mentorship can be quite valuable, particularly in helping people add some meat to their spiritual diet. But for all of their benefits, each of these is a limited vehicle.

Ultimately, this explains the diversified investments we see in the ministry of Jesus, as He worked with both crowds and individuals. But the limits of proclamation and mentorship also point to His emphasis on small-group discipleship through "the 12" as His key method to pursue Kingdom growth. From Jesus, we can confidently infer that small-group discipleship should be a significant piece of the puzzle.

Done well, small-group discipleship has most of the strengths of proclamation and mentorship, with less of their limitations. A small group is small enough to retain intimacy and relationship, to know what individual group members need, to model behaviors and attitudes well. It can be long-term enough to sustain life change. With more participants and more variety, it can be more interactive, with richer discussions based on a breadth of knowledge and experiences. It is still small enough where everyone can engage actively rather than be passive spectators. It is larger than a mentorship, allowing more lives to be influenced quickly.

Done well, small group discipleship will be more communal and relational than either mentorship or preaching. One can practice the "one another's" with mentors, but a larger set of peer relationships is more fertile ground for the rich community required to live out the Christian faith in different contexts. And the flexibility of a small group allows one to engage in all three models: small group leaders can engage in proclamation at times and meet with individuals to do mentorship.

"Equipping groups"

All of this assumes *effective* small groups—"equipping groups" that are centered on discipleship, growth, truth, love, etc. Many churches have small groups. But without a purpose centered on disciple-making, small groups can easily become social groups, devolve into heresy or small talk, rely on passive lecturing, settle for impersonal or short-term relationships, and so on. (See: Appendix 1 for "Twelve Tips" on how to run small groups more effectively.)

Some churches understand the theoretical value and importance of small groups for discipleship, but there is a lack of disciple-making purpose *within* their small groups. Who's leading the small groups? What do they know and what is *their* vision? What sort of oversight and training do they receive?

Small-group leadership can easily reduce to polite people who are willing to open their homes, use a good brownie recipe, collect prayer requests about second cousins and neighbors' dogs, play a DVD, and lead a tepid conversation where people share their opinions, tell long stories, and foist arcane Bible knowledge on each other. Maybe you've been in a group like this—or you've even led one?! Such groups are simply getting people together rather than reproducing disciples.

Other small groups are better by a notch or two. They discuss "hot topics," socialize and eat, share struggles and pray together, engage in acts of service, offer affirmation without much from God's word—all ok or even good stuff, but insufficient for robust discipleship.

Biblical teaching must be a significant part of the equation. Jesus modeled this for us, in demonstrating the value of meditating, memorizing, and using God's Word. Do you know that He used three passages in Deuteronomy to fend off the Devil's temptations in Matthew 4?! In sum, it's the Word of God, the Spirit of God, and the people of God. Without the Word and the Spirit, the people of God may be in a "small group," but it cannot be the meaningful discipleship of an "equipping group."

"Equipping groups" should have some length and aim for some rigor, but it's not merely about length or rigor. Curriculum and programs are fine, but for transformation, this must be done in the context of (committed) relationships. Small groups often pursue knowledge or relationship; to be effective, we must have both! Often, Type-A personalities lead and don't do much to intentionally develop new leaders or to be particularly relational. An "equipping group"—focused on making disciples and disciple-makers—must be Bible-centered and relational; intentional at striving for the goal of spiritual maturity; and transparent in following Jesus.

Another key goal is to move from knowledge transfer to the ability to "self-feed" and disciple others. You can sit in a small group for years and absorb some knowledge, but not be much better off in terms of a willingness and ability to share one's faith—or to answer tough questions about life. Equipping groups need to meet people where they are, but ultimately, the goal is to grow, learn, and stretch. Are the groups "meaty" enough? Does the environment or culture of the group encourage stepping out in faith, learning new things, getting empowered to lead and minister? Do the groups meet long enough and regularly enough to develop deep relationships, transparency, and biblical fellowship?

Preaching is limited in its influence and mentorship is limited in its numerical impact. So, effective small groups are probably necessary for a robust, multiplying ministry of disciple-making. Moreover, the strengths of small-group discipleship explain why Jesus embraced it so thoroughly. What did His ministry look like and what are the lessons for us?

Jesus and an "Equipping Group" Model of Ministry

Jesus had a plan and intentionally carried it out—and a big part of that was focusing His time and energies on a small band of disciples. Robert Coleman says:

> *At first glance, it might even appear that Jesus had no plan...This is one of the marvels of his strategy. It is so unassuming and silent that it is unnoticed...[when it] finally dawns on the open mind of the disciple, he will be amazed by its simplicity and will wonder he could have ever failed to see it before. Nevertheless...the basic philosophy is so different from that of the modern church that its implications are nothing less than revolutionary.*

Eugene Peterson observes that Jesus "restricted nine-tenths of his ministry to twelve Jews." Greg Ogden makes clear that Jesus did not depend on the crowds—and why: "Jesus didn't stake his future influence and kingdom on the groundswell of mass support. If he had, he would be a footnote in history grouped with other revolutionary leaders squashed under the Roman boot." Or applying the same logic to the miracles of

Jesus: if he had fed another thousand people with his feeding miracles, what difference would it have made?

We're here today—and the Church is thriving today—because of His investment in the 12. Let's look at the general stages of Christ's work with the disciples.

1.) "Come and See": Jesus started with an invitation to "come and see" (John 1:39). The disciples were asked to join Jesus as avid spectators—as He modeled the Spirit-filled life, engaged in ministry, and began to increase access to the Kingdom of God. The point was to illustrate what they would be joining—and to allure them into the attractiveness of a life sold out to obeying God's will and embracing His grace.

Here, we see Jesus working with those who had expressed interest. Perhaps they had heard about the miracle man from Galilee. Perhaps they were looking for the Messiah. Perhaps they had already had casual encounters with him. But He knew they had seen something and might be interested—and so, He extended the invitation.

Note the implied purposes communicated by the invitation—and then, throughout the relationship. There was a choice—to be in or not. (And many refused the offer—for a variety of reasons!) Those who said "yes" were coming to experience something worth seeing and replicating. They were being invited, at least eventually, into ministry—and away from a consumer mentality of religion. And the closed group of the 12 implied purpose as well: Jesus had a course of training in mind that would need to be completed, rather than picked up halfway.

2.) "Come and Follow": After some time, there was a second invitation—to "come and follow" (Mark 1:17; John 1:43). Jesus invites them to become "fishers of men" (Matthew 4:19)—an intentional, relational, and missional approach to ministry. Here, the disciples were formally invited into the group, asked to participate more fully, and provided with more explicit training. Presumably, Jesus perfectly tailored the wisdom and experiences for their level—stretching, broadening, and deepening them as they progressed.

Many of the relevant applications to ministry are obvious. Jesus narrowed His focus to a manageable number of disciples who would receive the lion's share of His efforts. The 12 received consistent, purposeful, and comprehensive training—over a long period of time. In a way, Jesus played favorites with the 12, giving them (far) more attention than anyone else. But that "favoritism" is the way in which training, parenting, coaching, and discipling can be effective.

Jesus would discuss things with His disciples, instead of merely lecturing at them. He was working on their heads, hearts, and hands. He was extending their knowledge, building their faith, and enhancing their humility. He was teaching them to be competent and instilling confidence as well—that through Him, great things could be done.

3.) "Abide in me; Bear Much Fruit": Near the end of His ministry, Jesus exhorted His disciples to abide in Him and to "bear much fruit…fruit that will last." (John 15:5,16) It's not that their training was over, but it would now mostly be on-the-job training. They were equipped for ministry and it was time to exercise those gifts and skills. They had seen, learned, and experienced enough to become fruitful ministers and ambassadors of the Gospel. As they engaged in ministry, they would exercise stewardship and dominion. They would learn from mistakes, stumbling but then getting back up (Proverbs 24:16).

As such, the disciples would grow in a different way—through the practice of their faith in the context of leadership and ministry. Often, we miss this step. People come out of one Bible study and immediately look for their next study. Churches offer study after study, led by the same people. There is little sense of direction or purpose—in essence, treating Bible study as an end, rather than as a means to (far) greater ends. The point of Bible study is to follow Jesus more effectively and to "go and make disciples." Participating in Bible studies can certainly help people grow. But thoroughly-equipped disciple-makers get to grow in a different and more profound way as they minister to others and make disciples—in many aspects of life and many realms of ministry.

4.) "So I Send You": Then, Jesus commissioned them with "so I send you" (John 20:21). He had already sent them out two-by-two (Luke 10:1). They had been active in ministry, under Jesus' wings. But now, Jesus released them to full-time service. From here, they would eventually go to the ends of the earth, empowered by the Spirit, inspired by Jesus and His model of ministry, fulfilling the Great Commissions, and living out the two Great Commandments.

For us, this implies a process which allows people to grow from spectators to ministry participants and then ministry leaders. This points to leaders who are willing to empower others and allow them to lead. It assumes effective shepherding as new leaders step into these roles. It requires equipping by the Spirit, but also times of general and specific training.

5.) "Come and Die": Finally, Jesus invited them to "come and die." As they fulfilled the Great Commissions, they would endure persecution and painful circumstances, faithfully following their Lord and His call on their lives. Another version of the disciple's initial call is Matthew 11:28-30—to accept the easy yoke of Jesus' sacrificial death. But the easy yoke then evolves into Matthew 16:24, with its call to "die daily and pick up one's cross."

We start with the crucifixion of Jesus as payment for our sins. But within sanctification, we have our own crucifixions—Galatians 5:24 (to the world) and Galatians 6:14 (to the sinful nature). Biblically, Christ's exhortation often led to serious decisions and profound consequences—from Abraham's willingness to sacrifice his only son to the martyrdom of Stephen. All of the apostles were willing to die for the Kingdom of Christ, the word of God, and the souls of men.

Some of us may be called to an explicit sacrifice. But all believers are called to be a persistent living sacrifice (Romans 12:1-2), daily crucifying ourselves to the World and the Sinful Nature. In this, through the Spirit, we are able to accomplish great things for the Kingdom—not just attending Bible study after Bible study, but engaging in ministry and leadership, making disciples and disciple-makers.

Chapter 5

Models in Ministry: Funnels, Chairs, and Discipleship

The harvest is plentiful, but the workers are few. Ask the Lord of the harvest, therefore, to send out workers into his harvest field.

—Luke 10:2

At first glance, it might even appear that Jesus had no plan…[but it] is so different from that of the modern church that its implications are nothing less than revolutionary.

—Robert Coleman

Forming people in Christ is a slow work, so it can't be hurried; it is an urgent work, so it can't be delayed.

—Eugene Peterson

As we discussed in the last chapter, preaching, mentorship, and "equipping groups" all have a place in disciple-making. Proclamation can be useful, but is quite limited. Mentorship can be effective, but can only help a few people at a time. Small groups (well-done!) have a number of big advantages for making disciples and disciple-makers. How can these methods attract people to the local church and disciple them once they're involved? How do we help others to roll up their sleeves?

Popular Models for Doing Church Today

Putman and Harrington describe four popular models of church ministry:

-***Educational:*** a focus on classroom methodology, where believers are built up in terms of Bible knowledge and life application

-***Attractional:*** a focus on entertainment, where outsiders are strongly attracted and insiders are held by "the show" at a corporate worship service

-***Missional:*** a focus on social justice and/or acts of service, with a wonderful emphasis on others, particularly the down-and-out and the oppressed

-***Organic:*** a focus on "doing life together," resulting in deep and abiding fellowship, and ideally, iron-sharpening-iron relationships

In all of these, there is usually a pastoral piece where professional staff "run the church", work to attract new sheep, and take care of current sheep. There is much to commend in all four models. But usually, something (big) is missing. For one thing, some of the pairings point to errors if they're not held in balance. Too much focus on "education" will not be "attractive", particularly in a post-Christian context. Too much focus on "attraction" may be a distraction to discipleship, resulting in a ton of shallow believers who are likely to fall away in an emphasis on quantity over quality. Too much focus on "missional" will be more social gospel than gospel. And too "organic" can be insular and otherwise limited.

In our church's context, we're prone to struggle with both parts of the first pair. Some of our folks put too much stock in Bible studies—studying as an end, rather than a means to greater ends. But we also aim to put on a great "show" (although we'd never call it that). A primary goal is to encourage attendance at church, particularly for those who haven't been to church in a while—or ever. Worship and other events are done with professional excellence. Such churches are "seeker-sensitive" in style and substance: casual in terms of dress and affect; striving to avoid boredom; addressing wounds and felt needs; providing good programming, comfortable seats, and aromatic coffee.

For any of these models, the great thing about Jesus' model of ministry is that if your church's primary focus is discipleship—well-defined and well-done—then they will reach all of these goals, indirectly. It may take longer, but the growth is on a solid foundation, rather than the shifting sands of entertainment, preferences, cultural fads, and felt needs. People will know the Scriptures and be *educated* on how to apply them to life. They will lead *attractive* lives, doing evangelism and ministry as a natural outpouring of what's in their hearts and heads. They will be *missional*, understanding the role of lifestyle evangelism and works of service to introducing people to Jesus. And their faith will be *organic*—inside and outside the church.

The Standard Funnel Model

A funnel is a useful way to model the approach of many churches. (***See: Figure 1*** on the next page.) They use weekend worship services to attract a lot of people, pouring them into the wide mouth of the funnel. The hope is that they'll move from the corporate worship service to smaller and deeper opportunities—serving within or outside the church, giving money, participating in Sunday School classes or community

Bible study groups. Hopefully, discipleship will occur as they move into the funnel. Hopefully, disciple-makers will eventually emerge through a long process of osmosis, as they absorb enough teaching, pile up enough faith and life experiences, and achieve enough spiritual growth to be helpful as competent lay ministers in the church.

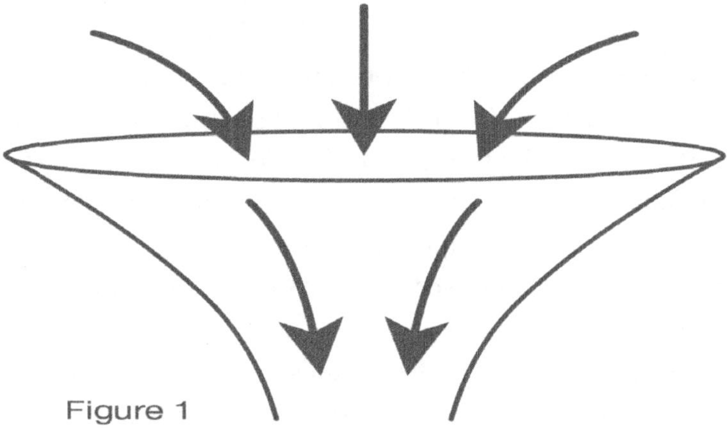

Figure 1

There are large costs and likely problems with this approach. First, for a great weekend worship service, it's important to have an effective and enjoyable sermon, inspiring worship music, an attractive setting, energetic children's programming, and so on. But it requires a lot of energy, resources, and talent to do these well. It's also common for all of this to devolve toward entertainment, passivity, and consumerism. If a preacher or worship leader is particularly gifted or tacitly sees himself as a performer, the temptations are even greater.

Second, at least implicitly, a funnel approach encourages a church to measure success as bodies, bucks, and baptisms. If so, we'll be more interested in how many people we have vs. how well they're growing. We may end up with a church-esteem built on numerical growth, instead of the increased faithfulness of disciples built on obedience to God's callings. We may get more excited about building projects than in building believers—a distorted "prosperity gospel" of sorts. Carlson and Lueken: "We live in a church culture where external success is self-justifying. If more people are coming to our church, this is obviously a sign of success, and God must be pleased." But clearly, there is much more to the Good News than growth in the number of reasonably well-behaved church attenders.

Third, a funnel may offer some opportunities for growth, but without sufficient intention for developing disciples and disciple-makers. It is challenging to come up with a model that lays out "next steps" for those who join a church. The next steps must be sufficient to cover the wide range of disciples within our stewardship and they should point to the goals within discipleship. And who will lead these next steps? The choices are to hire more staff or to develop lay leaders—ideally, thoroughly-equipped disciple-makers who have the skills, knowledge, wisdom, and vision to make disciples and other disciple-makers.

The Upside-down Funnel of Jesus

The other problem is that this approach to the funnel militates against the model established by Jesus. Oops! If one considers the ministry of Jesus, it is obvious that He spent time with the crowds and with individuals. But the bulk of His time was spent with the disciples—with the 3 (Peter, James, and John) and especially with the 12. Even when He was with the crowds and the individuals, He was usually with the disciples!

If it's generally a good idea to ask "What would Jesus do?", perhaps we should apply the question to our ministry and discipleship models as well. Jesus poured His life into the 12. His perfect efforts, along with the New Covenant and the empowerment of the Holy Spirit, are responsible for the survival, the growth, and the strength of the Church today. Think about how far the Church has come in 2,000 years!

Beyond the 12, we read about the 70 who were sent out two-by-two. We don't know a lot about them, but we can infer that Jesus poured into them too—not as much and probably in part, indirectly through the disciples. We also read about the 120 and the 500—again, groups not influenced as directly or as much by Jesus, but who still had value as workers in the Kingdom.

In Acts 2 at Pentecost, 3,000 converts "were added to their number." What happened to these new believers? We know they were absorbed into the life and community of the church. They didn't have a building that could handle 3,000 people—even with multiple services! Moreover, a preeminent focus on piling everyone into a big worship service was not consistent with the ministry model of Jesus. More likely, the 3,000 were mentored by the 500—perhaps in small groups meeting in homes and then in larger groups as possible. ***(See: Figure 2*** on the next page.)

Plateaus in the Funnel

The standard funnel model clearly falls short by implying that growth is both a smooth process and an inevitable result. First, if we put people in the top of a funnel, gravity should take them *naturally* from the beginning to the desired end. Second, a simple funnel implies *a smooth, consistent ride* from the one end to the other. In fact, neither is true.

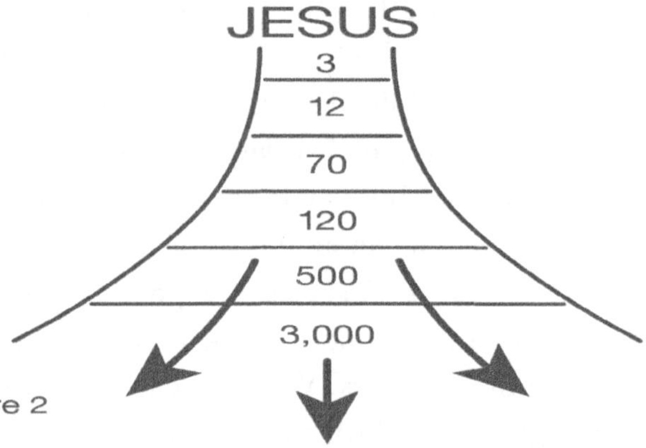

Figure 2

There is no inevitability to making disciples or disciple-makers. Discipleship and becoming a disciple-maker are far from a given. And assuming discipleship of some sort, the ends can vary tremendously. Disciple-making necessarily lends itself toward intentionality, focused effort, and vision. And we need to recognize the three big impediments to moving through the funnel—plateaus where one can easily get stuck and fail to make much additional progress. ***(See: Figure 3.)***

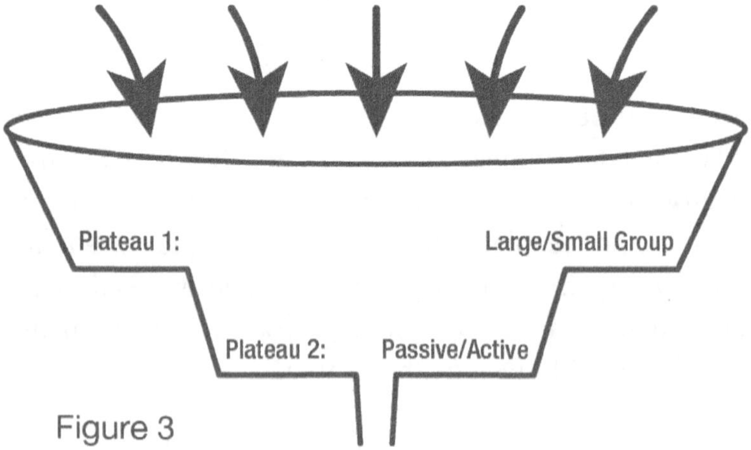

Figure 3

First, it is common for people to get stuck as a mostly-anonymous member of a large group—most notably, as an attendee at weekend worship services. Perhaps they reduce the Christian life to a weekly ritual. Perhaps they're afraid to risk the next step by trying a smaller group. Perhaps they're too busy and haven't heard or caught a vision for living out the Christian life in community, as a disciple of Jesus. Perhaps they're more interested in consumption of religious services than discipleship. Their progress in discipleship is anything but inevitable. In fact, leaving by the back door in a few months or a few years is more likely.

> ***If you're on this plateau, you need to get off the couch, roll up your sleeves, and get into a small group and/or a mentor/mentee relationship with a disciple-maker.***

Second, it is common for people to mostly tread water as a passive member in a small group—most notably, as a participant in a Sunday School class or community Bible study groups. At the less impressive end of this spectrum, they show up some of the time and participate little. At the more impressive end of this spectrum, they're regular attenders in a well-run group with a well-prepared teacher, participating in the sense of sharing opinions, providing input, and asking good questions. But their participation is limited to the meeting itself.

> ***If you're on this plateau, you need to roll up your sleeves and do something on your own—or ideally, in community. Read the passage from your pastor's sermon—once per day. Read a chapter of the Gospels each day and write***

down what God is showing you. Read a Christian book. And find others to join you!

A disciple is someone who takes some "ownership" in the process. As such, something more than attendance and passivity is required. Once people begin to do *something* outside of a meeting, they learn that greater growth is pleasurable and achievable on their own. Given the power of God's word and His Spirit within us, a discipleship process will pick up speed. From there, avid growth *is* much closer to inevitable—akin to the gravity of our original funnel.

As Howard Hendricks puts it: "Christian education today is entirely too passive. And that's incongruous, because Christianity is the most revolutionary force on the planet." He describes the "Law of Activity": "Maximum learning is always the result of maximum involvement" as long as the activity is meaningful. The implication and the goal? "Tell the learner nothing—and do nothing for him—that he can learn or do for himself...what's important is not what you do as a teacher, but what the learners do as a result of what you do...the ultimate test is not what you do or how well you do it, but what and how well the learner does."

We love the story about Bill Hull, who taught a university class and based each student's grade on how well they could teach someone outside the class—what Hull was teaching them inside the class. Each student was responsible to teach one person who would take the final exam for the student. Hull was communicating a key truth: it's not the student's knowledge as much as the student's disciple's knowledge and the student's ability to convey that knowledge in a process of multiplication.

Dealing with the Plateaus

So, it is important for churches to encourage people to move past these two plateaus—first, from large group to small group; and second, from passivity and attendance to activity and doing something *outside* the meeting. Churches often address the first plateau by offering various small groups. Dealing with the second plateau is far less common.

> ***But it's not only up to your church! If you take one thing from our book, it should be this: you must make investments in your own discipleship; you should do what you can to encourage others to do the same; and you should help your church offer people opportunities to invest.***

Small groups should be well-run with friendly people, interesting topics, service projects, and so on. But eventually, people should be called to small group participation with "homework": reading a book, journaling as they read chapters of the Bible, memorizing verses, accountability on evangelizing, practicing spiritual disciplines during the week, and so on—anything that gets them to do something *outside* the meeting. Once these two hurdles are overcome, people will almost always be on a path to rigorous discipleship—and eventually, disciple-making.

If you are stuck on either of these two plateaus, get yourselves plugged into your church's discipleship opportunities. If your church doesn't offer much, find some like-minded folks (and hopefully a godly mentor or two) and prayerfully find your own path. (We'll describe a number of options in Chapter 6.)

There is potentially a third plateau as well. Some people do years of *active* Bible study—not just attending, but participating and studying (hard) outside the meeting. But without more intentionality, the move from disciple to disciple-maker will still be far slower than it should be. People can get in a rut of seeking knowledge rather than applying it; "getting fed" far more than feeding others; and simply looking for the next study. We're not called *merely* to be disciples, but workers in the harvest and disciple-*makers*. A large set of Bible studies may do little to accomplish this goal. This requires a different vision: disciple-making is our calling; this is what God wants from us and for us. And it requires another sort of equipping—with a missional mindset, certain skills, and adequate confidence to be used effectively by God.

> ***If you're on this plateau, move from drinking to feeding others, from following to leading, from absorbing to passing it on. Get off the bench; grab a Barnabas to join you and a Paul to shepherd you; work with some Timothys; look to empower others; and see yourself as God sees you—a Kingdom worker who can make disciples who can make disciples who can make disciples.***

The "Four Chairs" model

Dann Spader's "Four Chairs" is a helpful framework for envisioning a disciple-making process. Churches should have a plan and a set of strategies for moving people through these four chairs in their discipleship with Jesus. Disciples should have a passion for discipleship and make the effort to move along the four chairs.

Chair 1 is "Win the Lost." The first priority is doing what we can to bring people into the Kingdom of God. We are saved by God's grace, rather than our works—but we're saved to do good works (Ephesians 2:8-10). This includes allowing God to use us to attract people to a saving knowledge of Him. As such, churches should have preaching, programs, and outreach events to help bring a variety of non-believers into relationship with Christ. And individuals should be equipped to evangelize a range of non-believers, from "random" to repeated encounters, from skeptics to seekers, from lifestyle evangelism to the ability to explain the Good News.

Chair 2 is "Build the Believer." Chair 2 believers are established and rooted in Christ; their identity is at least somewhat in Christ and they are empowered to some extent by the Spirit. They understand what they believe and why—to some degree. They are comfortable in the church, at least as a consumer. They are at least somewhat willing and able to do acts of service inside and outside the church. They'll invite people to church and may be able to share their faith. And so on.

But really, Chair 2 is more like a Couch in terms of its size. Its use ranges from new believers to those who have progressed a good bit in their faith. On the left-hand side of the couch, there are often passive recipients of Biblical wisdom from preachers and teachers. On the right-hand side, they are increasingly active in their faith and increasingly eager for more training and more ministry opportunities. For those who move along the couch, the more interesting question is the length of time it takes to make this progression. Is it a few years—and then moving on to Chair 3? Or is it a lifetime in Chair 2—someone who is not yet trained to be a Kingdom worker, despite years or decades in the church?

Chair 2 is also like a Couch in that it implies the potential for more comfort than a chair. A good couch is cozy—and especially as the cushions age, it can become difficult to "get off (or out of!) the couch." It's also good for naps—a nice feature of real couches, but an alarming temptation for our metaphorical, spiritual Couch.

Chair 2 is a part of natural spiritual growth. But the problem is that it can become the chair that believers occupy—comfortably, complacently—for their entire Christian life. Arguably, most people in the Church spend their life in Chair 2. The related problem for churches is that they must be purposeful to encourage the move to Chair 3. This requires casting vision, providing opportunities, and empowering disciples with skills and knowledge to become Kingdom workers.

Unfortunately, many churches offer little to get out of Chair 2. Their focus is often bodies, budget, baptisms, and buildings more than spiritual growth. The emphasis is on quantity far more than quality. Preachers put on and put out their Sunday best. Staff lead the ministries and "beat the bushes" to get enough volunteers. Spiritual growth is by happenstance or slow osmosis. Leaders give lip service to discipleship, but don't know where to start or are satisfied with Biblical preaching at a passive audience.

And often, church members are complacent as well—with little vision or passion for progressing. They are reasonably content but unaware of something greater—or quite willing to settle for something less. Or they're not especially content with their lives, but they don't connect a lack of discipleship to their problems. As we've described, all of this is insufficient for the task—and the opportunity—before us. What does it look like to move to Chair 3?

Chair 3 is "Equip the Worker." Moving beyond Chair 2, people in this chair have been prepared to be Kingdom workers. At this level, disciples are "correctly handling the word of truth," becoming lay ministers and shepherds. The faith of Chair 3 workers is largely self-motivated and self-sustaining. They still learn from the preacher and benefit from good teaching. But they are prone to engage in their own spiritual development. They will look for opportunities to minister to others—and empowered by the Spirit, will do fine work within the Kingdom.

Chair 4 is "Multiply the Overseers." These are disciple-makers who "multiply" ministries—overseeing leaders, shepherds, and participants. They can run ministries effectively or at least be team leaders. Depending on skills and temperament, they may be able to write curriculum, teach or preach, take the lead in establishing and running new ministries, and so on. They are go-to people who are eminently dependable, humble in spirit, fruitful in ministry.

Which chair best describes you?

Most church leaders are naturally drawn to evangelism and are usually willing to focus on getting people from Chair 1 to Chair 2. Ministry experience will further equip people who are in Chair 3. With some opportunities, experience, and a bit of training, Chair 4 people emerge naturally from Chair 3. The biggest challenge then, by far—and the Great Omission in much of the Church—is moving fans of Jesus into avid discipleship with Jesus, from Chair 2 to Chair 3.

Elton Trueblood notes that "Christ twice commanded His followers to pray for the emergence of a labor force, which was the obvious bottleneck of the new movement." And it's still the case today. It's often said that we shouldn't give a man a fish; instead, we should teach him how to fish. There is great wisdom in this. But for a multiplying ministry, one must go a step further: teach him how to teach others how to fish. How to do this? Through a range of purposeful opportunities that we'll describe in Chapter 6.

Chapter 6

A Range of Spiritual Growth Opportunities

All Scripture is God-breathed and is useful for teaching,
rebuking, correcting and training in righteousness,
so that the servant of God may be
thoroughly equipped for every good work.

—II Timothy 3:16-17

Christian education today is entirely too passive.
And that's incongruous, because Christianity is
the most revolutionary force on the planet.

–Howard Hendricks

The goal is rolling up our sleeves with respect to spiritual growth—not merely being more active at church, but "growing in the grace and knowledge of our Lord and Savior, Jesus Christ." (II Peter 3:18) Growth implies opportunities to pursue growth; an environment in which growth is fostered and celebrated; and disciples who have a desire to pursue growth. There's far more to spiritual growth and spiritual disciplines than study, but we're going to focus there for now. Why? Study should promote spiritual growth and point to other spiritual disciplines.

It's often said that service is the "love language" of God. More simply, Jesus said the two Great Commandments are to love God and to love others. To love God, we must strive to know Him better. Otherwise, we may passionately love a god who does not exist. To be effective in ministry, grace must be informed by truth. Otherwise, ministry can easily reduce to being nice to people. So, active participation in the will of God requires study, but goes far beyond study.

Despite the importance of "deeper" small groups, there is clearly a place for "lighter" small groups as well—as a way-station to something deeper. As such, a church should provide a range of opportunities—to address the range of disciples they will work with; to convey a process of disciple-making; and to impress the point that settling into a life of milk-drinking is not acceptable for a disciple of Jesus. If your church doesn't offer this, find a set of like-minded disciples and we'll help you get started in this chapter. (It's also important that small groups are run well. See: Appendix 1 for "Twelve Tips" on how to do this more effectively.)

A Full Range of Opportunities

A useful way to think about this is a spectrum of small group opportunities, ranging from 100 to 400 levels (akin to the organization of college courses). The following are generalizations for each category. But they provide a useful way to think about the range that should be offered to disciples and potential disciple-makers.

A 100-level group would be for seekers or new believers—something that invites them into the faith or engages them as novices in the faith. Group members would show up and receive relatively basic information about foundational truths and key life applications (e.g., marriage or personal finance). These could be small or large studies—making it easier for people to feel comfortable. (Larger studies might include a "non-threatening" small group component.) A leader might hope for some participation, but would not require it.

A 200-level group would target newer believers and those who have recently committed to a path of discipleship. The group would be smaller or at least have a significant small-group component. Leaders would strive for participation from everyone, but still without requiring it. The material would be obviously applicable (e.g., parenting, prayer, or lifestyle evangelism) and somewhat more challenging. Group members would be (strongly) encouraged each week to read from a light book or a few chapters from the Bible—or to memorize a Bible verse. (Simple "homework" would be provided with exhortations, but also with ample mercy and patience for those who struggle. One can imagine a spectrum of encouragement and exhortation here—as people are moving from milk to "yogurt" on their way to meat.) Outside of the group meeting, leaders would encourage members to put basic applications into practice—e.g., practicing solitude or how to pray with one's family. The small group component would provide some accountability, mentorship, prayer, fellowship, and a sense of living life together.

A 300-level study would attract those who have been on a path of discipleship and have moved from move from milk or yogurt to meat. The group would be small and intentional enough to get all members to participate, at least lightly. The material would be more challenging by another notch or two. Group members would be required to do significant work outside of the meeting—read a few chapters of a book, journal over many chapters of the Bible, memorize a Bible passage, etc. Outside the group, leaders would encourage members to put more challenging applications into practice—e.g., fasting or how to evangelize in a variety of settings. The small group component would provide significant opportunities for accountability, mentorship, and living life together.

A 400-level study would purposefully intend to make disciple-makers, to train up lay people to be "thoroughly equipped" workers in the Kingdom. (Some of this would occur in 200-level and especially 300-level groups, but the effort becomes more purposeful in a 400-level group.) This requires an intentional small group experience or mentorship. It requires rigor, time, and tons of Bible. It requires people to speak frequently, actively participating in the process. It requires experiential learning, knowledge of doctrine, wisdom on how to live life—along with competence and confidence to share all of this with others. It requires casting a vision for disciple-making, rather than focusing on the next Bible study they'll attend. (For us, this has been through DC—which we will describe later in this chapter—but there are other ways to accomplish the same goals.)

A few other thoughts. Remember that salt creates thirst and good food will stir an appetite. 200-level and 300-level studies will awaken a thirst for knowledge and growth—and an awareness of what disciples are capable of doing. 200-level and 300-level studies allow people to look in a mirror and see *for themselves* what they're willing to do. Moreover, it allows them to *signal* what they're willing to do. If your church offers a 400-level study without a 300 or even a 200, how will they know—and how will you know—if people are ready? One can use a "sink-or-swim" approach, but this causes all sorts of problems.

It's far better to offer a range of opportunities and encourage growth, slowly.

Group Level	**Material Type/Topics**	**Prep Time (hours) outside the meeting**	**Level of Participation within the meeting**
100	Basic truths and applications	0	Generally passive
200	Foundational theology and basic applications	0.5 – 2	Encouraged
300	Deeper theology and challenging applications	2 – 4	Strongly encouraged
400	Making disciple-makers	4 – 6	Mandated and equal

There are many analogies here. You can't run a marathon if you're a couch potato—or even, someone who takes the occasional jog. You can't bench-press your weight if you're constantly lifting sodas and snacks. You're unlikely to read a weighty 400-page book if you haven't turned pages in a decade. And so on.

Instead of the sink-or-swim of a diving board and the deep end of a pool, it's better to have the gradual slope of the entry into a wave pool. What is more likely to get believers out of their poolside chairs and into the water? We want them to enjoy the fun and adventure of the wave pool, with its risk and reward. A process which calls them to take small but manageable risks, to make modest investments, and to wade out into deeper and rougher waters. But instead of a wave pool—or even, the diving board and the deep end—many churches only offer a kiddie pool and a garden hose to get people wet in the waters of discipleship.

The farm system of a baseball team is also an apt metaphor: the Rookie League, Class A, AA, AAA, and finally the Major Leagues. Occasionally, players can "jump" to the Major Leagues, but usually a more gradual process is wisdom. As players progress, they get better at hitting the curve or throwing a slider. They improve at the fundamentals of the game, but over time, they gain experience against more challenging competition and situations with more pressure. The difference: only a few can be Major League baseball players. But everybody—with time and training—can be a Major Leaguer in the Kingdom of God.

Specific Examples of 200-Level and 300-Level Studies

There are many ways to do a 100-level approach and churches generally do these well. 100-level approaches are essential, but they can only take people a little way on a journey of discipleship—and should be seen, primarily, as setting the table for what should follow. In the next section, we'll describe the 400-level study we've developed in detail. So, in this section, we'll devote our efforts to describing a variety of 200-level and 300-level studies.

At the 200-level, there are two basic options: reading the Bible and reading Christian books. In terms of Bible reading, we recommend the practice of *lectio divina*. In a nutshell, it's a method or manner of reading the Bible and listening to what God is saying to you as you read it. *Lectio divina* has four stages: *lectio* (deliberate reading); *meditatio* (meditation on the passage); *oratio* (talk to God about the passage); and *contemplatio* (resting in God's presence).

In practice, *lectio divina* is best done with a Bible, a pen, and a journal or notebook. While one might come up with questions or learn a few things about a Bible story, the primary purpose is to reflect on God's word and apply it to your life. Read a passage and write down what the Holy Spirit is showing you. *Anyone* can do this!

Ideally, this should be done in community. For example, small groups might agree to read four chapters of Luke for six weeks—or read a chapter of Matthew each day over four weeks. Once a week—for accountability and edification—members would gather to share what the Lord has shown them. Choose wisely: Isaiah and Leviticus are terrific to study, but really tough to read. In the New Testament, don't *start* with Hebrews or any book after that!

Each participant would read the chapters, writing down reflections in a journal. Participants will benefit from sharing what God is doing with them, explaining the insights they have received, and receiving insights from others. It may be tempting to engage in tangential discussions—particularly on difficult topics or passages. But generally, the focus should be what each person received from God. ("Disciple Making Movements" [DMM] provides a useful format for this, reading a Bible passage in community, centered around ten basic questions—to connect with each other, to discover God's word and what it says to each person, and to hold each group member accountable.)

As Soren Kierkegaard expressed it: "How highly do you value God's word?" Imagine a lover who has received a letter from his beloved. I assume that God's word is just as precious to you…I assume that you read and think you ought to read God's word in the same way the love reads this letter." We tell people to read the Bible, but often, they don't know where to start or don't have the discipline to do it on their own. But it can be done if we come alongside of them with a plan and a community of like-minded disciples.

As for Christian books, there are many good options. You can cover specific, popular topics—e.g., parenting, marriage, and evangelism. You can read about more specialized topics—e.g., Garret Keizer's *Enigma of Anger*, Steve Arterburn's *Every Man's Battle*, or Cloud and Townsend's *Boundaries*. You can do a light discipleship curriculum, such as Francis Chan's *Multiply*. You can read provocative but small books—e.g., Robert Munger's pamphlet, *My Heart, Christ's Home* or two little books by Bruce Wilkinson, *The Prayer of Jabez* and *Secrets of the Vine.* You can cover basic theology—e.g., classic books such as Oswald Sanders' *Spiritual Leadership*, A.W. Tozer's *Knowledge of the Holy*, or J.I. Packer's *Knowing God.*

You can also read basic Bible commentaries that supplement your Bible reading—e.g., Warren Wiersbe or J. Vernon McGee. Or you can read books that more broadly supplement your Bible reading—e.g., Eric's book on Joshua (*Inheriting the Promised Land*) or Watchman Nee's book on Ephesians (*Sit, Walk, Stand*).

A leader (or two) should decide how many chapters to read each week. Leaders will facilitate the discussion, rather than "teaching" *per se*. They will hold group members accountable to do the reading (mid-week phone calls can be helpful!); encourage all to speak; and avoid tangents. (For a longer list of book possibilities, see: Appendix 2. We'll continue to update our list of 200-level and 300-level books at our website, ThoroughlyEquipped.org, under "Are you Ready for DC?")

300-level studies require more depth and length—a weightier approach and/or weightier topics. For example, you could do a modest discipleship curriculum—for example, our

Getting Equipped (DC28:20) Greg Ogden's *Discipleship Essentials*, or his work with Daniel Meyer, *Leadership Essentials*. They could read a single, thicker book such as Dallas Willard's *Divine Conspiracy*, John Piper's *Desiring God*, or G.K. Chesterton's *Orthodoxy*. Or they could read a series of related books on a certain topic or from a certain author. (Since 300-level studies are far less common and a bit more complex, we've provided significant details of their administration with some examples at ThoroughlyEquipped.org.)

Our two favorite examples are "An Intro to Spiritual Disciplines" and "An Introduction to C.S. Lewis". For the Spiritual Disciplines course, we take 13 weeks to read Dallas Willard's *Spirit of the Disciplines*, Richard Foster's *Celebration of the Disciplines*, and John Ortberg's *The Life You've Always Wanted*. Willard explains the "why" of spiritual disicplines; Foster explains the "how"; Ortberg is a simpler version of both. By way of analogy, Willard is salmon and steamed veggies; Foster is steak and potatoes; and Ortberg is pizza.

For the C.S. Lewis course, we take 12-13 weeks to read *Mere Christianity*, *Screwtape Letters*, *The Great Divorce*, and *A Grief Observed. Mere Christianity* is a classic of the faith—a good book to read annually. *Screwtape* is terrific on the subject of temptation. *Great Divorce* is a provocative book on Heaven and Hell—and its approach is a useful resource for apologetics in our post-modern era. And *Grief Observed* is Lewis' journal entries after his wife dies—a helpful perspective on what it looks like to earnestly and passionately wrestle with God in grief, especially for those who have not gone through it.

There are many ways to accomplish the goals of a 400-level. But there are only a few published options that provide a framework and curriculum to do so. Given the fruit that we've seen the Lord grant through our efforts, we're happy to recommend and describe our own 400-level work below—*Thoroughly Equipped: A Disciple-Making Curriculum*, or "DC" for short.

What is in "DC"? The Centrality of the Bible

The inspirational Joshua 1:9 is quoted often: "Have I not commanded you? Be strong and courageous. Do not be afraid; do not be discouraged, for the Lord your God will be with you wherever you go." But we forget what's written one verse prior: "Keep this Book of the Law always on your lips; meditate on it day and night, so that you may be careful to do everything written in it. Then you will be prosperous and successful." In part, the commanded courage comes from immersion in the Scriptures—and what it tells us about God's character and His activity in history.

II Timothy 3:16-17 says, "All Scripture is God-breathed and is useful for teaching, rebuking, correcting, and training in righteousness, so that the servant of God may be *thoroughly equipped for every good work*." The Bible is given to us by God and is eminently useful in all aspects of life—to "thoroughly equip" us to do all sorts of works. We are not saved by good works (Ephesians 2:8-9), but we are saved to do good works (Ephesians 2:10). How can we do those good works effectively if we fail to delve into the Scriptures through Biblical community?

In Acts 20:32, Paul connects knowledge of the word to spiritual growth: "Now I commit you to God and to the word of his grace, which can build you up…" Along the same lines, God's word is portrayed in Scripture as nourishment: bread (Matthew 4:4), milk (I Peter 2:2), meat (I Corinthians 3:2,

Hebrews 5:12-14), and honey (Psalm 119:103, Ezra 3:1-3). How can we fail to get our fill of the good food that God offers us?

As such, DC is a program of Bible memory, Bible reading, and Bible study. We believe that immersion in the truths of Scripture is a requirement for a Biblical worldview, significant discipleship, and fruitful ministry. DC requires about five hours per week of "homework"—reading through the entire Bible, memorizing key verses, and studying a wide array of topics from a biblical perspective.

Memory: Along the way, DC'ers memorize at least 70 verses of Scripture, putting God's word into their hearts, informing their prayers, their counsel, and their daily life. In most churches, Scripture memory is reserved for children. But why should they be the only ones who benefit from this spiritual discipline?!

Reading: DC'ers read the entire Bible over 21 months—read, not study. They read the Scriptures in a devotional manner, *lectio divina*, allowing God to speak to them through His word.

Study: There are many Bible studies that require this much "homework." But DC is different in that its goal is not to spend months tearing into a book of the Bible or a particular topic. This approach can be profitable; Eric has led such Bible studies for 25+ years! But our goal in DC is to develop lay leaders and to make disciple-makers. Pounding Romans or Isaiah for six months can be wonderfully edifying, but it won't do much to equip you to be a disciple-maker. A four-week study on spiritual gifts or evangelism techniques is a nice tool to have in your bag, but it won't lay the foundations for broadly effective ministry. If you're going to do that much work, we would encourage you to prioritize an approach that helps you grow in terms of systematic theology and developing a coherent and thorough Christian worldview.

What Topics Do We Study in DC?

DC'ers study an array of important topics, deepening a Biblical worldview, growing in their ability to live out the Christian life, gaining literacy on thornier doctrinal issues, and building the skills to wrestle appropriately with complex topics. In a nutshell, everything needed to be effective as a deacon or elder at a mid-sized church. The 21 months of DC include a survey of all topics that are relevant to lay leadership, ministry, and disciple-making. Of course, this same level of equippedness enables a DC'er to be effective as a Bible study leader, a junior-high group leader, a mentor—or outside the church, within a prison ministry, in a nursing home, and so on.

Rather than teaching one particular view on complicated, debatable topics, our approach is to expose people to the biblical case for the various views within Christian orthodoxy. Teaching and curriculum often reduce complex issues in an attempt to convince people of a single view. Instead, we want DC'ers to wrestle earnestly with these topics (perhaps for the first time), so they have more "ownership" of their views. More broadly, we want disciples to be able to think for themselves—and to feel confident as they go to the Scriptures and rely on the Holy Spirit.

We also want to equip DC'ers for evangelism, ministry, and discipleship—and to increase knowledge, humility, and empathy for those with different (but biblically acceptable) views. In other words, DC'ers learn a ton; they learn how little they know; and they learn how to use their knowledge effectively as they (more) humbly interact with others.

This is vital within the church—as we pursue true and robust unity. In His final words to the disciples before the crucifixion (John 14-17), Jesus repeatedly points to the importance of unity. Paul makes it his first topic in the application sections of Colossians and Ephesians. And it's obviously important as we interact with an increasingly post-Christian world, particularly in a time of heightened emotional sensitivities, increased "political correctness," and confusion about "tolerance." How can disciples develop tact, remain courageous, and be effective in the world?

Why Do We Study the Scriptures?

We study in order to…

—***become a strong and fruitful tree*:** Psalm 1:1-3 says "Blessed is the one who does not walk in step with the wicked or stand in the way that sinners take or sit in the company of mockers, but whose delight is in the law of the Lord, and who meditates on his law day and night. That person is like a tree planted by streams of water, which yields its fruit in season and whose leaf does not wither—whatever they do prospers." Water, roots, fruit, attractive, shade, and protection!

—***fight temptation*:** Psalm 119:11 tells us that God's word helps us avoid sin of all types: "I have hidden your word in my heart that I might not sin against you." Jesus modeled this for us. Most notably, in Matthew 4, Christ quotes Deuteronomy three times as He deals with Satan and severe temptation!

—***transform our mind and align it with God's will*:** Romans 12:2 points to the Scripture's part in this: "Do not conform to the pattern of this world, but be transformed by the renewing of your mind. Then you will be able to test and approve what God's will is—his good, pleasing and perfect will." All of Psalm 119 is an awesome reflection on God's word. But Psalm 119:105 talks about the Scripture's role in providing day-to-day direction: "Your word is a lamp for my feet, a light on my path."

—***defend ourselves and others against false ideas, philosophies, and worldviews*****:** Ephesians 6:17 reminds us to "Take the helmet of salvation and the sword of the Spirit, which is the word of God." And in II Corinthians 10:4-5, Paul writes: "The weapons we fight with are not the weapons of the world. On the contrary, they have divine power to demolish strongholds. We demolish arguments and every pretension that sets itself up against the knowledge of God, and we take captive every thought to make it obedient to Christ."

—***give a reason for the hope we have, dealing tactfully but truthfully with error and sin*****:** I Peter 3:15 says, "Always be prepared to give an answer to everyone who asks you to give the reason for the hope that you have. But do this with gentleness and respect..." Some of us struggle with truth; others struggle with love; we need both to be effective in God's Kingdom.

In Ephesians 4:20-22, Paul writes about the importance of teaching, truth, and *learning* a new "way of life." Of course, discipleship and "equipping" for ministry are not simply a matter of studying the Bible religiously. But II Timothy 2:15 says, "Do your best to present yourself to God as one approved, a worker who does not need to be ashamed and who correctly handles the word of truth." Ultimately, study enables us to grow in grace and knowledge, in doctrine and life—or it is worthless (or worse). "Do your best" does imply the need for diligence in our study. In II Timothy 3:10-14, Paul writes about life and doctrine—and then, roots them in the efficacy of the Scriptures in 3:15-17. One does not become a tree overnight or last for long with shallow roots.

Building Skills

After studying on their own for the week, DC'ers come together for a weekly meeting to discuss what they've learned—with facilitators co-leading the conversation. In DC's small group setting of 8-12 DC'ers, *everyone is required to speak about the same amount.* Big talkers are required to restrain themselves, to work on their listening skills, to "pick their spots" as they speak, and to give space for the quieter folks. The quieter folks are (gently) required to speak up, to come out of their shells, to find and develop "their voice," and to build confidence. If they can't learn to speak up in this setting, how will they ever share their faith with their neighbors and colleagues?

We also want DC'ers to work on specific skills that are useful for ministry and leadership.

—***Research***: Beyond *lectio divina,* DC'ers are also trained to dig deeper in the Scriptures, learning about the various genres in Scripture and how to do word studies. DC'ers do research on topics in cults of Christianity and world religions, key figures and moments in Christian history, and Christian denominations. If they encounter someone from an unfamiliar religion or denomination, they've had practice in figuring out the basics of those faiths.

—***Presentations***: DC'ers make presentations, learning how to research and organize short talks with hand-outs. This is an important skill for life and ministry—whether explaining the Good News or leading a devotional. We've even heard testimonies that God has used DC to conquer a fear of public speaking!

—***Teaching***: In addition to the brief presentations above, DC'ers read a short book by Howard Hendricks on teaching. They read the Scriptures for eight weeks through the mind of a teacher, preparing "mini-lessons"—the barebones of a lesson outline. And they teach a 25-30 minute lesson on one of the Ten Commandments. All of us are teachers at some level and we want DC'ers to have some practice in thinking like a teacher.

—***Service***: DC'ers engage in service projects with their groups. They learn how to serve more effectively. And if DC's educational emphasis tempts them to keep their nose in books, they're reminded that the Christian faith requires service, community, and reaching out to neighbors in love.

To reiterate, getting *everyone* to participate actively and *equally* in the weekly meetings is absolutely vital. In our trainings, we're fond of reminding co-leaders that we prefer a mediocre nugget from a quieter DC'er, rather than one more gold nugget from a talkative DC'er. If our top goal was knowledge dissemination, then Mr. Gold should do most of the talking. But our top goal is lay leadership development—and so, we need Mr. Quiet to talk…a lot!

Along the same lines, the presentations and the teaching opportunity serve to bolster these skills. Again, we're satisfied with a mediocre presentation if it sets the table for good presentations post-DC. As Hendricks notes: "Failure is a necessary part of the learning process." We don't *want* to hear a poor report or a mediocre lesson! But if that leads to competence or even excellence, the greater goal will be achieved.

Spirit-Led, Missional, and Relational

DC is Bible-centered and strives to be Spirit-led. Co-leaders are encouraged to work within a time framework, while allowing room for the Holy Spirit to lead the discussion. We have a Spiritual Disciplines retreat in the first ten weeks. DC has a 20-week focus on learning how to pray more effectively. The Bible reading is devotional in nature, listening to what the Spirit says as one reads through God's word. We teach on God the Holy Spirit—and the combination of God's provision and our participation in moment-to-moment life. We want DC to be educational and experiential. We want DC'ers to be filled with wisdom and the Spirit (Acts 6:4). We want DC'ers to be filled with the Holy Spirit and to speak the word of God boldly (Acts 4:31).

DC is study-centered and classroom-oriented, but it is also meant to be relational. DC'ers don't live together day-to-day. But they do walk beside each other—as brothers/sisters in Christ and as disciples of Christ—over 21 months. For many people (especially men), DC is life-changing as a first opportunity to build really significant and even life-long friendships. The existence of such relationships is itself life-changing. But in many cases, it stirs a new imagination for the sort of friendships that one should pursue.

More profound relationships—and a vision for the same—is a secondary goal or a by-product within DC. Likewise, we like "accountability," but find it more fruitful in settings where relationships develop naturally and where accountability can develop organically. Of course, it helps that people in DC are generally on the same page in terms of their desire to grow in grace and knowledge. So, this common pursuit often paves the way for effective accountability.

Another fruit of DC is mentoring—by co-leaders and/or by other DC'ers. Key individuals have played an important role in our lives. And we've mentored other individuals, including opportunities through long-term, rigorous, small-group settings. DC can be reduced to its educational component. But it's meant to foster deep and abiding relationships between people in the roles of Paul, Timothy, and Barnabas.

DC is not explicitly "missional"; we don't have a particular series of lessons on the concept. But the first two memory verses help to convey a missional mindset from the beginning. II Peter 3:18 has the awesome exhortation to grow in grace and knowledge. And in Ephesians 2:10, we're told that we're God's masterpieces, created to do good works, to partner with God in ministry. From there, "missionality" is infused through the curriculum and the process. DC instills or deepens a missional spirit by developing competence and confidence to do ministry. Through the empowering they receive, DC'ers catch or extend a vision to empower others.

For those who might have trouble finding appropriate "next steps" in ministry, we have an event where we cast vision and lay out some potential avenues for ministry. Without this, we've equipped but not empowered; we've built competence but not confidence; we've acquired knowledge without a passion to share it; we've grown in love and grace without the means to love our neighbors.

Along the same lines, one might reasonably worry that "going deep" will be more about intellectual strength and a narrow approach to morality. But with the power of the Word of God, the disciplines inherent in DC, and the competence and confidence developed by DC'ers, most of our "graduates" become far more effective and more missional in the missions to which they've been called. They do learn a ton, but they grow in humility and a passion for ministry and evangelism—far better equipped and ready to be used more effectively by the Lord.

DC Co-leaders and Shepherds

Kurt and Eric have only led about 50 DC graduates since we started in 2002. The other 2,200+ graduates have been led by co-leaders and shepherds that we've trained and shepherded. And now, those DC'ers are ministering in the church and in the world, empowered to do great things in God's Kingdom. We can't disciple thousands of people effectively, so it has been awesome for God to allow us to develop a multiplying ministry, so others can lead thousands!

Our co-leaders build up tremendous skills and knowledge—often with little previous leadership experience. We've found co-leading a DC group to be a particularly effective way to develop new disciple-makers. They've gone through DC for 21 months, learning and experiencing a ton. After a break of three months (or longer if they move into other ministries for a season), they can go through DC as a co-leader. The workload is about the same, but the learning curve is different—and in some ways, steeper.

Looking at the ministry of Christ in developing the disciples, Matthew 10 (Mark 6, Luke 9) indicates that He started slow and didn't expect much. He did not allow them to go beyond Israel to Samaria or the Gentiles. Such a task would have been too challenging at that point. He allowed them to heal people (a great opportunity to serve), but greatly limited their preaching. As A.B. Bruce notes wryly, we're "tempted to wonder how Christ could trust them to open their mouths at all." The results were apparently modest, but the effort was repeated later with considerable success.

For us, DC co-leaders "start slow"—as participants in DC. But then, as co-leaders, they *really* learn the material—and continue to grow in seeing the Bible and relationship with God as a deep well. They have the opportunity to establish and maintain a disciple-making culture as a leader. They learn how to handle difficult moments and conversations—inside and outside the weekly meetings. They get to practice this and see it modeled for them by the shepherds who are doing likewise with them! They grow in their dependence on God and in their small group management skills. They minister to DC'ers as if they were the deacon of a small church. And they become more and more missional. All of these are excellent opportunities for immersion in the lifelong work of making disciples and disciple-makers. It is vital to put developing leaders into positions where they can learn and experience these things.

More broadly, disciples and disciple-makers need competence and confidence, skills and vision, grace and truth, wisdom and courage, a Spirit-filled and Spiritually-disciplined life. They increasingly become workers who do not need to be ashamed and who correctly handle the word of truth. They also learn how to make mistakes in a safe environment; it is important to learn from failures in ministry. They learn how to deal more effectively with authority, peers, and those they're serving. They become progressively better at handling problems with wisdom and tact, with grace and truth, with courage and discernment. As Robert Clinton quips: "Problems are God's stepping stones to maturity." All of these are excellent training opportunities for disciple-making—in whatever context God leads them.

Our experience has been the same as Bill Hull's: "After being a member of the discipleship group for two years and then leading for two years, the trained disciple maker has had the time to own the principles, skills, and convictions concerning the disciple-making process." In our experience, after the 42 months, we've found that our co-leaders can do just about anything in terms of Kingdom work.

Final Thoughts on Vision and Equipping

Equipping people for every good work is the goal. Making disciple-makers will grow the church—effectively. Disciple-makers have a vision and heart to be missional and the knowledge, skills, and experience to be Spirit-led and effective. One cannot do this well without competence and confidence.

All of this is unlikely to take place unless someone in your church has a vision—and an effective plan—for making disciples and disciple-makers. Biblically, the primary job of church leaders is to equip others to do ministry, expanding the outreach of the Kingdom (Ephesians 4:11-16). Instead, church leaders are often focused on the Sunday service, running the church, and ministering to the needy. If they're distracted by these good pursuits, *you* need to pursue the greater things, finding like-minded disciples and prayerfully finding your own path of discipleship with Jesus. Roll up your sleeves and get ready for action!

We have a vision that most believers can be fruitful as Kingdom workers, and can lead in various ministries—whether up-front or behind the scenes, whether before large groups or mentoring one-on-one. It's inspiring to see existing Kingdom workers sharpened by DC. They were active and effective, but DC changes the direction of their ministry or makes them more effective. Better yet, the Lord uses DC to allow many people to transition from solid citizens in the church to Kingdom workers. They've been on the back bench of the church for years. After DC, they emerge as new leaders in the local church and the Church, able to make a far larger difference for the Kingdom of God.

In all of this, we want DC'ers to be widely competent, rather than competent to lead people through a particular book or method. We want DC'ers to have a I Timothy 3 / Titus 1 lifestyle, whether they ever hold the office of elder or deacon. Although some DC'ers will lead others through DC, the vast bulk will move into other forms of ministry, making a difference in the lives of others—all over the church and throughout the community. DC grads are "thoroughly equipped"—in a deep but general sense—to do ministry of a variety of sorts. Our goal is not to multiply DC, but to use DC to multiply disciples and especially disciple-makers—wherever they are in the Kingdom.

Chapter 7

Conclusion: Opportunities and Challenges

When they saw the courage of Peter and John and realized that they were unschooled, ordinary men, they were astonished and they took note that these men had been with Jesus.

—Acts 4:13

We have generated a body of people who consume Christian services and think that this is Christian faith.

—Dallas Willard

As we wrap things up, we hope that you have a vision for becoming a disciple and a disciple-maker—that these pursuits are both desirable and feasible. We have laid out the general characteristics of what it takes to make that vision happen—and provided a number of specific opportunities. Hopefully, your church has good "next steps" in place for you. If not, you can find some like-minded disciples and a mentor or two—and find a clear way forward. As you roll up your sleeves and walk this path, you will increasingly become ready for action!

What's at stake here? Not just your individual walk with Jesus. Not just the legacy for your children and grandchildren.

Not just the healthy growth of your local church. But also, the growth of God's Church and the expansion of His Kingdom.

Hope for a "New Reformation"

The Reformation was a long-simmering effort to correct aspects of the Catholic Church's course—against misconceptions of God and abuses by church leaders. It promised that priests would no longer obstruct the people of God; instead, there would be a "priesthood of believers." Religion would not be a compilation of rules and rites in an institutional setting; instead, it would be based on a personal relationship with God through the Bible and His people.

Hendrik Kraemer describes the reforms of the Reformation: a condemnation of the Pope's hierarchical authority, a return to salvation by grace alone, the preeminence of the Scriptures, and the priesthood of all lay people—"the laity." Kraemer writes: "And yet, it must be frankly stated that neither this new conception of the Church nor this strong vindication of the laity has ever become dominant…To the present day, it rather fulfills the role of a flag than of an energizing, vital principle."

As Greg Ogden observes, Luther, Calvin, and other Reformers…

> *promised to liberate the church from a hierarchical priesthood by rediscovering 'the priesthood of all believers'. But the Reformation never fully delivered on its promise…Within Protestant circles, we are fully acquainted with the first aspect of the priesthood of all believers…all believers have direct access to God through Jesus Christ…The unfinished business and the unkept promise that has the power to unleash a grass-roots revolution in the*

> *church is the logical corollary to the priesthood of all believers: not only are all believers priests before God, but we are also priests to one another and to the world.*

In this, Ogden notes a painful irony: "Protestant churches have been just as priest-ruled as Catholic churches, we just call it by a different name." As we celebrate the 500th anniversary of the Reformation, how far have we really come? The good news: "We live in a generation when the unfinished business of the Reformation may at last be completed."

Ogden points to many causes for the current state of affairs and the forsaken promises of the Reformers. For example, he devotes a chapter to church-speak. "Saints" are considered to be spiritually elite, rather than a label for every believer (as is the case throughout the New Testament). We refer to "the ministry" as if it's the particular province of professionals—and to "the minister" of Church X as if church members are *not* ministers of the Gospel. We call the professionals by formal titles like "reverend"; we designate "the clergy" as a leadership caste of specialists. They dress in clerical garb and preside over various sacraments. All of this serves to separate "them" from "us," at least in practice.

Another example: Since Kurt moved from being the pastor of a satellite campus to full-time parachurch ministry, his kids are often asked "Is your dad ever going to pastor again?" And their children blurt out: "He pastors every day!" It's not helpful—to professionals or to lay people—to think of "ministry" in such narrow, purely-professional terms.

Even in traditions with fewer rites and speakers in more casual clothing, the "us and them" distinction still holds, more or less. We depend on professional staff more than lay pastors.

We tend to see evangelism as inviting people to church, so they can hear the Gospel—rather than something we can do well with the Holy Spirit, as we walk daily with Jesus. We focus on conversion and baptism over "teaching them to obey everything" Jesus has commanded, forgoing purposeful and robust discipleship within biblical community.

The "Laity Advantage"

The funny thing about all of this is that the laity naturally have a tremendous advantage and greater opportunities—as lay people. How often do professional ministers try to do ministry in the world and are hamstrung when people find out that they're professionals? There are definite advantages to being a lay ambassador for the Kingdom, including this lack of stigma. As Kurt likes to joke, he's paid to be good, but Eric is "good for nothing." As such, the laity should be seen as *subjects* and *agents* of ministry, rather than merely as *objects* of ministry. After all, the Lord's Prayer opens with "our Father" and a universal desire that we all voice to see God's Kingdom "come".

On the one hand, people sometimes have an inappropriate view of ministers—that they are the *only* people who can minister—for example, demanding that a professional take care of funerals, counseling, mentoring, and hospital visits. On the other hand, lay people doing such work effectively can be really powerful. The lay person has another potential advantage in that he is closer to "everyday" life in the world and will see things from a fresh (non-professional) perspective.

Of course, all of this assumes the competence of lay people to do ministry—which begs the question we've tried to address in this book: how do we get lay people thoroughly equipped for these opportunities? Elton Trueblood notes that "The layman often has a signal advantage in the ministry…but this initial advantage will not carry him far unless he has something important to say and unless he learns how to say it effectively."

At one level, the goal is negative—to prepare lay people so they can avoid trouble. Trueblood again: "The best insurance against falling away is the development of a profound and well-grounded set of convictions…Ushering on Sundays and singing in the choir will not, in the long run, be substitutes for genuine conviction." But it is not a sufficient vision for lay people to stay out of trouble and minister mostly by asking people to church or trying to push their questions to a professional pastor.

Even in the Christian-friendly 1950s, Kraemer pointed to advantages that the laity can have in the world—"where the real battles of faith are being fought." But he observed that too often, they feel "spiritually powerless and illiterate." What to do? "It is just on the point of enabling the laity to account for the hope and the faith which is in them that the theologians have to meet and strengthen the laity…For the laity should in this matter not be seen primarily as the needy, ignorant, and helpless, but as that part of the Church that has to carry the brunt of the burden of encounter with the world."

Consistent with God's persistent desire to empower, it is His desire for each of us—professional and lay person—that we have as much power as we can handle. As Dallas Willard puts it:

> *Great power requires great character if it is to be a blessing and not a curse…it is God's intent that in his kingdom we should have as much power as we can bear for good…the intention of God is that we should each become the kind of person whom he can set free in his universe, empowered to do what we want to do…But character, the inner*

directedness of the self, must develop to the point where that is possible.

Christian Consumerism

Willard points to a Christian consumerism: “We have generated a body of people who consume Christian services and think that this is Christian faith.” One suspects that this is the larger issue. We are often training Christians to be consumers, not disciples. How can we plant so many seeds of consumerism and expect the fruits of discipleship? Carlson and Lueken: “Attracting people to church based on their consumer demands is in direct and irredeemable conflict with inviting people, in Jesus’ words, to lose their lives in order to find them.”

In his study, “The State of Discipleship”, George Barna finds that pastors don’t intend to feed the monster of consumerism. *Only 1%* of senior pastors and discipleship pastors thought “today’s churches are doing very well at discipling new and young believers.” More optimistically, 8% thought *they* were doing “very well” and 56% thought they were doing “somewhat well.”

Barna also finds a staggering chasm in the *perceptions* of the discipleship efforts offered by the local church. In contrast to pastors, *92% of church members* surveyed thought their church “definitely” or “probably” does a good job! And 38% preferred to “disciple on their own”—as if that’s a viable option! All of this points to incoherence about discipleship from lay people—and vast room for improvement on vision and strategy from leadership.

This can lead to immense challenges for pastors who want to emphasize discipleship. Carlson and Lueken describe their own church's difficult transition from a "seeker sensitive" church to a model that emphasized discipleship:

> *We broke an unwritten contract we had with our congregation...we provide people with programs and weekly services that satisfy their religious needs and preferences, and they continue to attend and support the church with their time and money...We discovered that people weren't necessarily coming to church to be formed in the image of Christ...More sobering is the extent to which we had oriented the church around the concerns of those who were minimally interested in being apprentices of Jesus.*

Jesus faced a similar moment in John 6. After miraculous healings and a free meal, the crowds were attracted to His work, but not a path of discipleship with Him. Jesus gave them a tough message the next day, saying among other things, that he was the Bread of Life. But most of them were only interested in the free bread and a good show. It can be the same today. If few people have a vision that discipleship is desirable and feasible, then church leaders will need to make that case—and may find it difficult to lead consumers down this path. Still, the effort must be made: a large church of consumers is not consistent with the Great Commission or making disciples who live on the Bread of Life.

"My people won't do that much work!"

Similarly, pastors often worry along these lines: "If I ask them to do anything, I'll lose them or nobody will show up." We think they would probably be surprised. They have people—like you—who would be willing and able to step up and do something right now.

As for our capstone course, we often hear this: "DC sounds great. But they study five hours per week? For 21 months? I don't have *anyone* who would do that!" Maybe they're correct in that many of their people are not in good enough shape to do DC—right now. They haven't heard the vision; they haven't built up much muscle in terms of spiritual disciplines.

Starting DC might be akin to asking couch potatoes to run a marathon. But that only begs the question of what couch potatoes are capable of doing—with vision and training. Again, you start with modest training and build up from there. In our experience, when people begin to make small investments, they often catch the vision and eagerly make greater investments. Bill Hull observed, "The higher we set the bar, the hungrier they became."

Another challenge in this regard is that our culture has moved away from reading to some extent. A reliance on technology—from its distractions to its emphasis on the quick and ephemeral—is not helpful to our goals. The good news, at least for now: young people have recently been students in school and older people are usually not as enamored with the new technology.

In any case, this can be overcome. For many people, completion of DC largely requires saying no to TV. If one has a daily hour of TV to drop, DC is rather easy to do. In any case, if we're "people of the word", if the Bible has immense value for life, if God's revelation has value for all time, then we need to find a way to make this—or something like this—happen. What's your plan? What's the alternative?

Two Stories to Close

Let's close this out with two stories of the many we could tell—one about an individual who was discipled from a knucklehead to a Kingdom worker, and another about a historic church recovering from a long slow fade, thanks to a purposeful investment in discipleship.

The first story: Before we had produced many disciple-makers through DC, Dick wanted to fast-track Gary into a leadership position in Men's Mentoring. Kurt met with Gary and asked some tough questions, but Gary handled this poorly. So, Kurt said that Gary would need DC and then training to serve in Mentoring. This infuriated Gary, revealing to Kurt that he had made the proper decision!

Later, Kurt went to pray for someone else at a retreat and saw Gary's name on the list. Kurt decided to go to Gary's room and pray for him as well. Gary was broken by the experience, admitted his sin of bitterness, and repented. Soon afterward, Kurt invited Gary to participate in Men's Mentoring and to join DC. Gary went through DC and has been an effective leader ever since—in mentoring and prison ministry. Although a longer process, it was far better than putting him into leadership too soon. Investing effectively to grow purposefully is the more-fruitful approach.

The second story: For decades, South Louisville Christian Church (SLCC) had been the catalyst for starting every "independent Christian" church in Louisville, including our home church. But in recent decades, SLCC had fallen on hard times: changing demographics, an aging church body, and church leadership not investing in new leaders. The church was old and dying. Theo Dues was the new pastor—his first pastorate. He realized that he must invest in new, younger leaders if the church was to survive, or even thrive again.

In October 2009, Theo heard Kurt and Eric speak at a conference. Then, Eric met with Theo in January. Theo was convinced that DC was the ideal process for him to pursue. But he didn't have the leaders to spare to run DC groups at SLCC. So, Eric sent out an email to all local, former DC co-leaders, asking for volunteers to train up DC'ers for 21 months at SLCC. Seven men stepped up from various local churches, willing to drive some distance to another church to serve their people and develop new lay leaders through DC. In Fall 2010, a group of ten men started with two co-leaders from different churches. And in May 2012, seven men graduated—all lay leaders now, including two new deacons and their first new elder in 30 years! Today, SLCC is vibrant and growing again.

Theo tells a story, saying that he asked God for growth at SLCC. He felt like God said to him, "What would you do with them if I sent them?" Theo realized that he did not have the Kingdom workers and the "infrastructure" to handle many new members, responsibly. After the first DC groups—and the DC groups that have followed among men and women—he has that in place, increasingly.

Great things can happen for you—and within your church—even among those who are not yet competent to be Kingdom workers. But to get there, we must embrace a vision for making disciples and disciple-makers; we must raise the bar for ourselves and those in our circles; we must lay out a coherent plan for disciples to deepen their walk and become disciple-makers; and we must pursue those plans with passion and perseverance.

Our Good and Great God wants to partner with us in ministry. Let's get off the couch, roll up our sleeves, and work on getting thoroughly equipped. Let's grow (quickly) in grace and knowledge. As God's workmanship, let's get ready for action—for the works He has already prepared in advance for us to do!

Appendix 1

Twelve Tips for Running an Effective Christian Small Group: An "Equipping Group"

Let's start by defining some of the terms. First, "effective" depends on your goals. Our goal is to make disciples and disciple-makers—disciples who can make disciples. So, what are your goals and how can a small group discussion be most effective in promoting these goals?

Second, a "small group" is anything between, say, 5-20 people. The first of two huge barriers to fruitful discipleship—the plateaus in our funnel from Chapter 6—is getting people to move from a large group format (e.g., worship service) to a small group format. How effective are you at overcoming this barrier?

Third, a "Christian" small group requires something beyond the merely social (although it also includes a significant social element). A *Christian* small group implies a significant study piece—whether book or video, whether the Bible, a book by a Christian author, or even a secular book studied from a Christian perspective.

Fourth, an "equipping group" should have the explicit goal of strategically and aggressively moving from Chair 2 to Chair 3, from disciple to disciple-maker. This speaks to the second barrier/plateau: some equipping can occur through passive spectatorship, but equipping will accelerate tremendously as people make investments (e.g., through study, service) outside of merely showing up and meeting together.

The following comments are aimed at the discussion piece of a Christian small group for disciples—or an "equipping group" that intends to build up disciple-makers.

1.) Learn people's names within the first meeting if possible. Take pictures, study their names, pray over your group members. In a group of modest size, there is no excuse for not knowing their names after you've met them once.

2.) There's far more to an effective small group than simply the discussion! In terms of making disciples and disciple-makers, it is crucial to reach head, hands, and heart—to convey knowledge and to model behavior; to love and serve people within the group in addition to teaching and exhorting them; and so on. Exhort people to put principles into practice, addressing both heart and habits.

3.) Encourage them to do something more than just show up. The second (and most over-looked) barrier to effective discipleship is "moving past passivity," especially outside of the group meeting. In lighter groups, "homework" should be encouraged. (For example, if you're covering John 9 next week, suggest that they read it multiple times and journal about it.) In heavier groups, homework should be required. Don't fool yourself—or them! Your people simply cannot progress quickly if they don't put time and energy into their own discipleship. Just showing up to hear a bunch of sermons or even an excellent small group teacher is far from sufficient for even modest growth.

4.) Less of you / more of them. Get group members to talk as much as possible. Unless you're a riveting speaker, discussion will be (far) more interesting. And in any case, they'll take greater ownership in their faith and the process of discipleship.

5.) Get comfortable with silence. Wait for them to answer; be patient. Take a breath—and then re-word the question if necessary. If you wait, they'll (almost always) say something useful.

6.) Aim for balanced talking among group members. In more elementary groups, this should be a goal. In more advanced groups, insist on it. Encourage quiet people to speak—and then encourage them when they have spoken. Privately or publicly, encourage more talkative people to take it easy and pick their spots. This allows more room for the quieter folks. And it allows the talkers to work on skills they need to develop: listening, patience, and empathy. In a word, it's usually better to hear a mediocre nugget from a quiet person than one more strong comment from a big talker.

7.) Ask lots of (good) questions. Emulate Jesus who asked 301 recorded questions in the Gospels. (Eric taught a series on this; if you'd like the notes, email him at DSchansb@ius.edu.) Avoid yes/no questions. Avoid questions with obvious answers or regurgitations of what they've just read. As useful, write out questions beforehand.

8.) Be careful with the length and type of your replies to their responses. Use non-verbals as much as possible; you don't need to say something every time. Use verbal replies that vary from quick affirmation to lengthy engagement. It is common for leaders/facilitators to talk too much after too many comments from group members. Avoid this temptation. Remember: every minute you talk, you're not allowing them to talk and "find their voice."

9.) Avoid tangents. You have more important things to discuss, right? Limit their tangents tactfully. (Have a public or private discussion about this if useful.) And you should rarely if ever *create* tangents. Don't cause trouble you're trying to prevent—and don't be in the business of modeling the creation of tangents!

10.) Organize your notes effectively. Experiment until you find a system that works well—and then continue to tweak it. It's common for people to have too much stuff in their notes. The good news: it's all in there; the bad news: you can't find it easily. Try a basic outline format with indents for sub-points. Try single words, phrases, and clauses—instead of sentences. Only use sentences for things that you need to word carefully or when you're using a quote.

11.) Make a schedule. First, publicly commit to a start time and (at least an approximate) end time. Then, have a rough timeline for what you hope to cover in a given time frame (e.g., Ephesians 1:3 in a Bible Study—or Ephesians 1-3 in DC Bible Reading—from 7:15-7:25). Generally stick to the schedule, but be flexible as you learn how to do this well—and after that, as the Spirit leads you to adjust.

12.) Work toward empowering others to teach and lead. Find aspects of a week's meeting that a novice can lead—the opening prayer, compiling prayer requests, introducing visitors. For more-experienced disciples, give them something more challenging—e.g., leading part of a discussion. For those with the competence to do so, work with them to lead an entire week. All of this requires more work on your part; it's easier just to do things yourself. But it is an important step to empower others.

Appendix 2

Potential Books for Small Group Studies

200-level books

-Arterburn: *Every Man's Battle*

-Bonhoeffer: *Life Together*

-Bridges: *Pursuit of Holiness*

-Chan: *Forgotten God*

-Cloud & Townsend: *Boundaries*

-Corbett & Fikkert: *When Helping Hurts*

-Eldridge: *Wild at Heart*

-Epp: *The Other Comforter*

-Goetz: *Death by Suburb*

-Halter: *Flesh*

-Halter: *Tangible Kingdom*

-Hammond: *Sentness*

-Hirsch & Frost: *Shaping of Things to Come*

-Hurnard: *Hinds' Feet on High Places*

-Idleman: *Not a Fan*

-Idleman: *Gods at War*

-Jones: *The Path*

-Keller: *The Meaning of Marriage*

-Keizer: *The Enigma of Anger*

-Leithart: *A House For My Name*

-Leithart: *The Four*

-McManus: *Uprising*

-Miller: *A Praying Life*

-Moore: *Onward*

-Munger: *My Heart, Christ's Home*

-Murray: *Two Covenants*

-Nee: *Normal Christian Life*

-Nee: *Sit, Walk, Stand*

-Ortberg: *Everybody's Normal Till You Get to Know Them*

-Ortberg: *Soul Keeping*

-Osborne: *Accidental Pharisees*

-Packer: *Knowing God*

-Platt: *Radical*

200-level books (cont'd)

-Ripen: *Insanity of God*

-Runyan & Pathak: *The Art of Neighboring*

-Sanders: *Spiritual Leadership*

-Sauder: *God Seekers*

-Sauder & Schansberg: *Enough Horses in the Barn*

-Schansberg: *Inheriting the Promised Land*

-Silvious: *Foolproofing Your Life*

-Sjogren: *Conspiracy of Kindness*

-Smith: *The Christian's Secret of a Happy Life*

-Smith: *You Are What You Love*

-Sproul: *Holiness of God*

-Sproul: *Reason to Believe*

-Stanley: *Choosing to Cheat*

-Stanley: *Next Generation Leader*

-Strobel: *Case for Faith*

-Strobel: *Case for Christ*

-Stuart & Fee: *How to Read the Bible For All Its Worth*

-Thomas: *Saving Life of Christ*

-Tolstoy: *A Confession*

-Tozer: *Knowledge of the Holy*

-Tozer: *Pursuit of God*

-Voskamp: *1000 Gifts*

-Voskamp: *The Broken Way*

-Ware: *The Man Christ Jesus*

-Whitney: *Praying the Bible*

-Whitney: *Spiritual Disciplines for the Christian Life*

-Wilkinson: *Secrets of the Vine*

-Wilkinson: *Prayer of Jabez*

-Wilkinson & Kopp: *Dreamgiver*

-Willard: *Renovation of the Heart*

-Woodward: *You Shall Know the Truth*

-Yancey: *Soul Survivor*

-Yancey: *The Jesus I Never Knew*

300-level books

-Bailey: *Jesus Through Middle Eastern Eyes*

-Bonhoeffer: *Cost of Discipleship*

-Bruce: *Paul: Apostle of the Heart Set Free*

-Chesterton: *Orthodoxy*

-Friesen: *Decision-Making and the Will of God*

-Grudem: *Systematic Theology*

-Jersak: *Can You Hear Me?*

-Keller: *The Reason for God*

-Luther: *Small Catechism*

-McManus: *Artisan Soul*

-Murray: *With Christ in the School of Prayer*

-Nouwen: *The Inner Voice of Love*

-Piper: *Desiring God*

-Reeves: *Delighting in the Holy Spirit*

-Sauder & Schansberg: *Getting Equipped (DC28:20)*

-Schlossberg: *Idols for Destruction*

-Tripp: *Instruments in the Redeemer's Hands*

-Willard: *Divine Conspiracy*

On occasion, we'll update this list at our website, ThoroughlyEquipped.org, under "Are you Ready for DC?"

Selected Bibliography

Bruce, A.B. 2010. *The Training of the Twelve.* ReadAClassic.com.

Carlson, Kent and Mike Lueken. 2011. *Renovation of the Church: What Happens when a Seeker Church Discovers Spiritual Formation.* Downers Grove, IL: IVP Books.

Clinton, J. Robert. 2012. *The Making of a Leader: Recognizing the Lessons and Stages of Leadership Development, 2nd ed.* Colorado Springs: NavPress.

Coleman, Robert. 1987. *The Master Plan of Discipleship.* Grand Rapids, MI: Revell Books.

Coleman, Robert. 1993. *The Master Plan of Evangelism.* Grand Rapids, MI: Revell Books.

Crabb, Larry. 1995. *The Silence of Adam: Becoming Men of Courage in a World of Chaos.* Grand Rapids, MI: Zondervan.

Gallaty, Robby. 2013. *Growing Up: How to Be a Disciple who Makes Disciples.* Bloomington, IN: Cross Books.

Hawkins, Greg and Cally Parkinson. 2007. *Reveal: Where Are You?* Barrington, IL: Willow Creek Association.

Hendricks, Howard. 1987. *Teaching to Change Lives: Seven Proven Ways to Make your Teaching Come Alive.* Sisters, OR: Multnomah Publishers.

Hull, Bill. 2004. *Choose the Life: Exploring a Faith that Embraces Discipleship.* Grand Rapids, MI: Baker Books.

Hull, Bill. 2007. *The Disciple-Making Pastor: Leading Others on the Journey of Faith.* Grand Rapids, MI: Baker Books.

Kraemer, Hendrik. 1957. *A Theology of the Laity.* Philadelphia: Westminster Press.

Luck, Kenny. 2012. *Sleeping Giant: No Movement of God without Men of God.* Nashville: B&H Publishing Group.

Ogden, Greg. 2003. *Unfinished Business: Returning the Ministry to the People of God.* Grand Rapids, MI: Zondervan.

Ogden, Greg. 2003. *Transforming Discipleship: Making Disciples a Few at a Time.* Downers Grove, IL: InterVarsity Press.

Pope, Randy. 2013. *INSourcing: Bringing Discipleship back to the Local Church.* Grand Rapids, MI: Zondervan.

Putman, Jim and Bobby Harrington. 2013. *Discipleshift: Five Steps that Help your Church to Make Disciples who Make Disciples*. Grand Rapids, MI: Zondervan.

Sauder, Kurt and D. Eric Schansberg. 2017. *Enough Horses in the Barn: Thoroughly Equipped Disciple-Makers and the Ministry of Jesus*. Louisville, KY: Further Still Ministries.

Spader, Dann. 2014. *Four Chair Discipling: Growing a Movement of Disciple-Makers*. Chicago: Moody Publishers.

Trueblood, Elton. 1967. *The Incendiary Fellowship*. New York: Harper & Row.

Trueblood, Elton. 1952. *Your Other Vocation*. New York: Harper & Brothers.

Wilkins, Michael. 1992. *Following the Master: A Biblical Theology of Discipleship*. Grand Rapids, MI: Zondervan.

Willard, Dallas. 1998. *The Divine Conspiracy: Rediscovering our Hidden Life with God.* San Francisco: HarperSanFrancisco.

Willard, Dallas. 2006. *The Great Omission: Reclaiming Jesus's Essential Teachings on Discipleship*. New York: HarperOne.

Willard, Dallas. 1988. *The Spirit of the Disciplines*. New York: HarperCollins.